The Pastor as Prophet

The Pastor
as Prophet

EDITED BY

Earl E. Shelp
and
Ronald H. Sunderland

The Pilgrim Press
NEW YORK

The scripture quotations are, unless otherwise indicated, from the *Revised Standard Version of the Bible,* copyright 1946, 1952 and © 1971, 1973 by the Division of Christian Education, National Council of Churches, and are used by permission. The scripture quotation marked TEV is from *Good News for Modern Man,* the *Today's English Version of the New Testament.* Copyright © American Bible Society 1966, 1971. Used by permission.

Library of Congress Cataloging in Publication Data
Main entry under title:

The Pastor as prophet.

"Originally presented as the Parker lectures in theology and ministry at the Institute of Religion in Houston, Texas"—Acknowledgments.
Bibliographical notes: p. 169.
1. Pastoral theology—Addresses, essays, lectures.
2. Clergy—Office—Addresses, essays, lectures.
3. Prophecy (Christianity)—Addresses, essays, lectures.
I. Shelp, Earl E., 1947– . II. Sunderland, Ronald, 1929–
III. Title: Parker lectures in theology and ministry.
BV4017.P26   1985   253   84-26534
ISBN 0-8298-0547-8 (pbk.)

The Pilgrim Press, 132 West 31 Street, New York, NY 10001

Contents

Acknowledgments

The essays that compose this book were originally presented as the Parker Lectures in Theology and Ministry at the Institute of Religion in Houston, Texas. The financial support by friends of Mr. R.A. Parker, for whom the annual series is named, is gratefully acknowledged. The encouragement of Dr. David Stitt, then director of the Institute of Religion, and the institute's Board of Trustees also deserve recognition. The contributors, who not only produced manuscripts, but also gave stimulating and provocative oral presentations, should know of our appreciation for their labors. Audrey Laymance carefully prepared the manuscripts for publication. We thank her for her assistance. Without her contribution the lectures and essays could not have taken this form. Finally, we express gratitude to Marion M. Meyer of The Pilgrim Press for her interest in and loyalty to this project.

By calling attention to the prophetic task we do not mean to suggest that pastoral ministry is reducible to this function. Subsequent lecture series planned by the Institute of Religion will examine the priestly and servant dimensions of the pastoral office.

The Pastor as Prophet

CHAPTER 1

Prophetic Ministry: An Introduction

Ronald H. Sunderland and Earl E. Shelp

Pastoral ministry is a theological activity. This statement appears unchallengeable. Yet a review of training for pastoral ministry in the decades from the 1930s through the 1970s demonstrates how tenuous this claim had become. Practical theology was peripheral to the concerns of academic theologians, and the pioneers of practical theology, in the form of "the pastoral care movement," turned away from biblical and theological studies to the social sciences to justify their emphases.

Representatives of these two branches of theology—"academic" and "practical"—are beginning to recognize that both must take account of the concerns of the other, in order to fulfill their separate and joint mission.[1] This collection of essays contributes to the emerging conversation and recon-

Ronald H. Sunderland, Ed.D., is professor of theology and ministry at the Institute of Religion, Houston, Texas.

Earl E. Shelp, Ph.D., is associate professor of theology and ethics at the Institute of Religion, and assistant professor of medical ethics at the Baylor College of Medicine, Houston, Texas.

ciliation by examining the prophetic task of pastoral ministry, a theme still largely overlooked.

That there has been a gulf separating academic and practical theology can be demonstrated by a review of pastoral education since the 1930s. But to focus on pastoral education alone is too narrow an emphasis, when one is aware of the broader context, namely, the response of the religious community to the cultural challenges occasioned by the scientific-industrial revolution. One dilemma for the religious community that resulted from the scientific revolution was that of defining the relationship of theology to secular disciplines. Science has been strident in its rejection of religious dogma, forcing religion on the defensive. It is therefore ironic that scientists should now, with such rigidity, insist that their dogmas should be accepted unquestioningly. With respect to the behavioral sciences, the response from representatives of the Christian community was to develop new theological inquiries that exploited the expanding boundaries of the emerging social sciences. Edward Thornton has traced the impact of medicine and social work on education for pastoral ministry in the 1920s and 1930s.[2] Asking how one may account for the attraction of medicine and social work for clergy in the twenties, he answers in the words of Helen Frances Dunbar, M.D., who chaired a Joint Committee on Religion and Medicine within the Public Health Relations Committee of the New York Academy of Medicine in 1929. In her first annual report as medical director of the Council for the Clinical Training of Theological Students in 1930, she said: "Today it is the priest (i.e., pastor) who is coming to be suspect and ostracized from the increasingly large social groups. . . . If the priest is to be restored to his place in a populace which has imbibed deeply the scientific method, he must drink at the same well."[3] Such terms as "Pastoral Psychiatry,"[4] "Pastoral Psychology,"[5] and, eventually, "Pastoral Psychotherapy" became current in the literature of pastoral theologians, as they

4

sought to introduce research from the social sciences into education for pastoral ministry.

During the 1940s and 1950s, attention was focused on the emerging field of pastoral counseling as a specialized aspect of pastoral ministry. This concentration tended to emphasize the bond between pastoral theologians and the behavioral sciences. Thus, Wayne Oates stated in 1957 that "personality theory is at the crossroads today. Both theologians and psychologists stand at the intersection. Their interests converge and separate at the point of identifying the religious dimensions of personality."[6] Carroll Wise also reflects the extent to which personality theory influenced education for clergy who engaged in pastoral counseling. Noting that "the Christian faith has not produced a workable theory of personal growth," Wise dismissed as a "misunderstanding" the criticism that the pastoral care movement was too much involved with Freudian theories.[7] He went on to emphasize the movement's strong theological roots, which, however, did not preclude the need for pastors "to have an appreciation of the work of the leaders in the behavioral science fields."[8] The literature of Oates, Wise, Seward Hiltner, and others during this period played a large role in shaping the nature of education for pastoral ministry and defined the scope of that ministry.

This trend served the Christian church well. Theological education benefited from the movement, both with respect to the content of curricula and from the respect of those theologians and social scientists who approved the efforts to bring theological education into the twentieth century. But this development was not without cost to theology and theological education. In the process of integrating the insights of the behavioral sciences with pastoral education, the theological distinctiveness of the church's unique pastoral concerns was placed in jeopardy. Despite affirmations to the contrary, the criticism continued that the pastoral education movement remained too closely wedded to the behavioral sciences and did

5

not draw sufficiently from its theological roots. The criticism was applied particularly to the newly emerged pastoral counseling movement.

In 1974, Henry Cassler, president of the Association for Clinical Pastoral Education, called pastoral educators to rediscover their theological roots through a more disciplined relationship with the respective denominational structures and their seminaries. This call to rediscovery was reinforced in 1975 by Cassler's successor, William Oglesby, who issued a similar challenge. On the occasion of the fiftieth anniversary of the clinical pastoral education (CPE) movement in the United States, Oglesby stated his conviction that association members needed to focus their continuing education on the theological dimensions of their task. Quoting Anton Boisen, one of the founding fathers of clinical pastoral education, he said: "We are trying to call attention back to the central task of the Church, that of saving souls, and to the central problem of theology, that of sin and salvation."[9]

More recently, James Wharton echoed the warning and the challenge. He argued that it is urgent for people who engage in pastoral ministry to do so on the basis of the faith commitments of their respective communities. He continued:

> Nothing is more destructive to the practice of ministry . . . than the vague (or not so vague) conviction that the genuinely helpful things undertaken are actually based on disciplines that lie outside the domain of faith and theology. When that conviction is sufficiently strong, members think of themselves as not-quite-honest or not-quite-qualified psychologists, social workers, or sociologists. . . . Even stout and clear convictions about what one does as a minister are difficult to maintain in the face of popular opinion that ministers are at best second-stringers in the scientifically grounded arts of helping people.[10]

Wharton's essay was the first in a series of lectures commissioned by the Institute of Religion in 1978, under the general rubric of "Theology and Ministry." The lecturers were invited to examine the extent to which both Jewish and Christian scriptures may inform the nature and scope of pastoral ministry in the United States in the 1980s and 1990s. In addition to a biblical examination, a more historical-theological approach was already being formulated: To what extent does the traditional formula of the ministry of Jesus as prophet, priest, and servant inform pastoral ministry in the congregation and in the church at large? This book is the proceeds of the first of three projected lecture series and addresses the first function: To what extent is pastoral ministry to be prophetic in nature and expression? Or, more explicitly, can the church's pastoral ministry be effected validly unless it is informed by prophetic concerns? What is the relationship between public ministry and pastoral ministry, to recall Donald Browning's question of the mid-sixties.[11]

Browning's agenda in 1967 was to respond to the rebuke issued by theologians and "the prophets of public ministry," who were inclined to see pastoral care in terms of community organization, and who accused pastoral counselors of being unconcerned with the societal ills that lay behind many individuals' needs for such counseling. Counselors were assumed to be supporters of the status quo by default and to be primarily dedicated to the reduction of conflict, internal and external. Thus, pastoral counseling "seemed irrelevant, if not actually dangerous, to the central strategy of those most actively engaged in public ministry."[12]

One important aspect of Browning's article was the recognition that the two functions of ministry—prophetic and pastoral—had been sundered into two "movements," neither informed by the other. The "social justice" movement scoffed at those clergy who were perceived to be disinterested in social and political reform, while many pastoral practitioners, including parish clergy, dismissed the former as radical reformers who succeeded only in polarizing the religious and the secular communities—a disservice to both! We believe that the urgency for conversation between pastoral ministry and classic theological disciplines[13] is equaled by the need for

7

conversation between proponents of pastoral ministry and proponents of public ministry.

Our concern is more comprehensive than that of Browning. The question of the relationship between prophetic and pastoral ministry must now be addressed to the life and ministry of each congregation, as well as that of the church at large, and not be limited to the field of pastoral counseling as only one aspect of pastoral ministry. In what manner ought the congregation's pastoral ministry be informed by its prophetic nature and purpose? Can the congregation's pastoral ministry be understood apart from the church's prophetic message— and what would be the impact on the shape of that ministry if it were so informed?

The assumption of the prophet's mantle is usually accompanied in scripture by a marked degree of ambivalence, for all but the foolish recognize that the prophet often becomes the target of a community's anger. To state what one's hearers do not want to hear is to invite rejection, while to fail to address sensitive issues forthrightly is to evoke indifference and scorn. Jesus reminded his disciples that those who followed him could expect not merely derision, but active opposition (Matthew 10:21–22). Prophets usually are not welcome in their own communities—or, indeed, elsewhere.

Yet the term prophet appears in the traditional model that delineates the role of the Christian pastor who seeks to emulate the threefold ministry of Christ as prophet-priest-servant. The question arises as to whether this archetype is of more than mere passing interest to clergy who are called to the ordained ministry of the Christian church. The authors of these essays believe with the editors that the prophetic ministry of ordained pastors as prophets is not merely an option, still less an idle curiosity; it is incumbent on them as an important feature of their role and identity.

Before this inquiry is addressed further, there must be some common starting point from which to examine the nature and scope of prophetism, both in a biblical sense and in the context of the contemporary community's perception of the prophetic role. First, the prophets experienced their respective calls as leaving them no option; they were obliged to obey a God who loved Israel to the utmost, but whose love was always experienced in the setting of justice and power (e.g., Ezekiel 3:12–16; Amos 7:14). The prophets experienced themselves as sent from God, with a special message or mission from God. Second, there was a well-developed moral content to their pronouncements in God's name regarding "the consequences of Israel's disobedience; the political situation and the call to dependence upon the Lord; true religion contrasted with the cult and sacrifices; and injustice and oppression of the poor by the wealthy and powerful."[14]

In the Christian scriptures, Jesus is the prophet par excellence. His ministry and message were directed to Israel as the community of faith (Matthew 10:6; 15:24), as those of the prophets before him had been. Like his predecessors, he reminded the nation of its obligation to the widow, the orphan, and the stranger—the technical and legal categories identifying those in the community who were "outside the system" and whose needs constituted a special claim on the community. Like the ancient prophets, Jesus faced the unremitting hostility of the representatives of the system, who had failed to keep covenant with God because they had failed to discharge their covenant responsibilities to the defenseless poor.

The witness of the prophets was powerful, because a message that was vital to the health and stability of the nation was proclaimed forcefully, often dramatized by the use of startling symbols that reinforced the message. It was usually societal rather than individualistic in scope, meaning, and significance. The power of the prophetic message was in its source, its truth, not in the charisma of the speaker. Thus, Isaiah drew attention to the danger of a strong alliance with Egypt and Ethiopia, which were threatened by the growing belligerence of Assyria. The prophet saw that Assyria would

9

conquer the two countries and that nations allied to them would also fall. His warning was disregarded, so for three years he dressed as a slave, walking the streets of Jerusalem "naked and barefoot" (Isaiah 20:1–6). This passage is an example of "the symbolic actions by which the prophets sometimes drew attention to and declared the 'word' which they felt called upon to utter"[15] (see also Jeremiah 27—28 and Hosea 1:1–3). Isaiah's action highlights one aspect of the prophet's method, that is, a willingness to be exposed to ridicule and injury. "A man with a mission does not hesitate to accept scorn or derision in doing his duty."[16] In the jargon of the 1980s, "the prophets did what they had to do."

The prophets also realized that symbols could be misunderstood and misused by false prophets or by political administrators who were anxious to shore up their own positions (e.g., 1 Kings 18:30). Jeremiah invoked the holiest of symbols, the temple, reminding his hearers that merely to shout "the temple of the Lord" would not bring about righteous living or their own salvation. Micah warned Israel that the traditional symbols—thousands of rams, or ten thousand rivers of oil—were meaningless if the people failed to act justly, to love steadfastly, and to walk wisely before their God. The prophets created new symbols in the place of those that had been emptied of value and meaning—new symbols that announced that *all* were invited into newness of life, to know *shalom*, to experience hope as the foretaste of coming reality. Thus, Hosea took as his wife "a worthless woman" (1:1–3), their children's names representing both the judgment and the promise of God to Israel. Amos' symbols were the plumb line and a basket of summer fruit; the meaning was the same (7:8; 8:1).

But the biblical picture is complicated. There were "true" prophets and "false" prophets. The distinction was critical, for false prophets misled the people and evoked God's wrath (e.g., Jeremiah 23; Ezekiel 13; Micah 3:5). Jesus was familiar with the work of such prophets who "come to you in sheep's clothing but inwardly are ravenous wolves [Matt. 7:15]." Although it is not within the purpose of these essays to pursue this aspect of the discussion, the issue is as critical for the religious community today as it was for Jesus and for the Israel of Jeremiah or Elijah. How does one identify the "true" prophet? The following essays suggest at least one answer: The true prophet speaks with the heart of a pastor and with the passion of one who has seen and felt the pain and suffering of the dispossessed, the helpless, and the disenfranchised. The true prophet's denunciation has the force of righteousness to the extent that it is born out of care—both for the oppressed and for the oppressors.

Second, the prophets' statements and actions, with the force of truth behind them, not only proclaimed judgment on existing outworn, inhuman, unrighteous forms, but also gave witness to alternative forms that summoned the nation to actualize truth, justice, and equality and to speak of peace in place of fear. We live today in a world in which ethnocentric pride is elevated by fear and hostility, such that fear of the stranger is found everywhere. In addressing this concern, Jürgen Moltmann suggests that alienation "becomes dangerous and destructive when its potential for anxiety and aggression is directed toward the construction of systems of mastery, exploitation and oppression."[17]

It is against such systems that the religious community is called to speak with a prophetic voice as a symbol of God's pastoral intent toward a common but deeply divided humanity. In the period before the 1984 Presidential election, "stereotyping the Russians" became a favorite ploy of the Reagan Administration, aided by the Moral Majority. President Reagan offered Americans "the solution to a vexing theological debate: he had discovered 'the focus of evil in the modern world.' . . . Monsters, godless barbarians, the Russians lurk at the edges of darkness. They are moral exiles."[18]

11

And for such an evil nation, no painful end could be too terrible. Had the command of Jesus to "love your enemies" been forgotten?

The Talmud expresses vividly the recognition that the divine way is not the human way. Remembering that Proverbs 24:17 instructs Jews not to "rejoice when your enemy falls," one Midrash pictures God rebuking the ministering angels who "wanted to chant their hymns [at the destruction of the Egyptian army in the Red Sea (Exodus 14:16–31)]: 'The work of my hands is being drowned in the sea, and you shall chant hymns?'" "The Holy One, blessed be He, does not rejoice in the downfall of his children," noted the Talmud writer.[19] For, to employ unashamedly an anthropomorphism, God is at heart one who ministers to the whole creation, because God loves and has compassion for every creature, without the limitations by which we humans so readily discriminate between "goodies" and "baddies."

The Talmudic story dramatizes the relationship between pastoral and prophetic ministry that is the theme of these essays. Speaking or acting in the name of the community of which she or he is a member, the pastor-prophet offers a response necessitated by a deeply felt pastoral need. It was because the king had failed to protect the widow and the orphan or had substituted potentially destructive political judgments for God's word, that the prophet felt called to summon king and nation to forsake injustice and to live "rightly."

These images are familiar to the pastor, the ready content of sermon and Bible study. What relevance do they have for parish clergy and the pastoral ministry of the congregation in the eighties and beyond? One has only to reflect on the public ministry of representative pastors and congregations in a multitude of settings to acknowledge that, whereas Browning's 1967 critique may have been justified with respect to pastoral counselors, it does not do justice to the work of many clergy and congregations. A dramatic recent illustration was the ac-

12

tive participation of countless parish clergy and laypeople in the civil rights movement.

The linkage of the pastoral image with that of the church's public, or prophetic, ministry was implicit in the message of Martin Luther King Jr. In an address delivered at Riverside Church in New York City, on April 5, 1967, sponsored by the Clergy and Laymen Concerned About Vietnam, Dr. King likened the use of new U.S. weapons on peasants in Vietnam to the Germans' testing of "new medicine and new tortures in the concentration camps of Europe." "If America's soul becomes totally poisoned, part of the autopsy [report] must read 'Vietnam,'" he said. He recommended to preachers that they "awaken the conscience of the nation" to what he termed the evils of the Vietnam conflict.[20]

This same witness to the inseparability of prophetic and pastoral ministry is replicated endlessly at the local congregational level and in the life of the church at large. A widely publicized current event has been the "Pastoral Letter on War and Peace," issued on May 3, 1983, by the National Conference of Catholic Bishops in the United States.[21] Many denominations have issued similar statements at the national, regional, and local levels, some calling for unilateral nuclear disarmament, others calling on the Administration to renounce both the possibility of a "first-strike" action and the concept of limited use of nuclear weapons. The pastoral letter was marked by the strong moral tone of the Hebrew prophets and the language was consistent with the just-war theory:

> Offensive war of any kind is not morally justifiable . . . ; it is never permitted to direct nuclear or conventional weapons to "the indiscriminate destruction of whole cities or vast areas of their population . . . "; the intentional killing of innocent civilians or non-combatants is always wrong. . . . No defensive strategy, nuclear or conventional, which exceeds the limits of proportionality is morally justifiable.[22]

The May 3 letter was followed by the appearance of Archbishop Joseph L. Bernardin (Chicago) and Archbishop John

13

O'Connor (New York) before the House of Representatives Committee on Foreign Affairs on June 26, 1984. They stated that their testimony was intended to sharpen the focus and refine the position of the Roman Catholic bishops on nuclear war. They challenged the efficacy and wisdom of deployment of the MX missile system and linked that decision to general arms control. In Archbishop Bernardin's words, "We use this Congressional testimony to call for a new effort of political will and creative diplomacy on behalf of a new round of super power negotiations to reverse the arms race."[23]

The 1983 pastoral letter affirmed the bishops' agreement with the Vatican Council II's assessment that "the whole human race faces a moment of supreme crisis in its advance toward maturity." Their statement was based on the conviction that "faith does not insulate us from the challenges of life; rather, it intensifies our desire to help solve them precisely in the light of the good news which has come to us in the person of Jesus, the Lord of history."[24] Through the resources of faith and reason, they added, they wished their letter to provide hope for people and direction toward a world freed from the nuclear threat. They expressed the hope that their pastoral letter would make a contribution to the wider public debate in the United States on the dangers and dilemmas of the nuclear age.

By the very nature of their statement, the bishops linked their prophetic concern to the church's pastoral ministry. Noting that the biblical texts do not address specific questions such as that raised by the threat of nuclear war, they urged that the scriptures do provide immediate direction when read in the light of today's concrete realities.

> The fulness of eschatological peace remains before us in hope and yet the gift of peace is already ours in the reconciliation effected by Jesus Christ. These two profoundly religious meanings of peace inform and influence all other meanings for Christians. Because we have been gifted with God's peace in the risen Christ, we are called to our own peace and to the

making of peace in our world. As disciples and as children of God, it is our task to seek for ways in which to make the forgiveness of God visible in a world where violence and enmity are too often the norm.[25]

Patrick G. Coy, in a commentary on the links between the bishops' action and that of Martin Luther King Jr., noted that, as the bishops had done, "King spoke out of a particular context: he was an American pastor who cared deeply about the soul of his nation." Just as the bishops point to U.S. responsibility for the arms race in calling for unilateral initiatives by the United States, King had singled out U.S. responsibility for the Vietnam war. In the mid-sixties, opposition to the war was extremely unpopular. Coy notes that "given all these considerations, King's action was reminiscent of the bold steps of the Hebrew prophets. It stands as a prophetic challenge to other American pastors now grappling with a Christian response to the arms race."[26] Such a prophetic voice, then, as now, deserves a hearing only if it is spoken out of a deep sense of pastoral concern not only for people as individuals, but for the whole creation as well.

Prophetic pastoral concern, when exercised by the National Conference of Catholic Bishops or by a charismatic leader like King, is very much in the forefront of public attention—and that has its own symbolic significance in a nation now deeply polarized. But much prophetic ministry that is essentially pastoral in intent is often quiet and unobtrusive, because the actors are seeking to respond faithfully in action and word to the gospel and would be content without achieving public notoriety. Such events have occurred in connection with the provision by congregations of sanctuary to refugees from Central American countries. Fully aware of the implications and probable consequences of their actions, congregations have acted because of their pastoral compassion for refugees. That their ministry would bring them into conflict with federal authorities was recognized as a secondary, and prophetic, ministry—but this result was neither wished nor courted.

On June 27, 1984, Stacey L. Merkt was sentenced to two years of probation for transportation of three Salvadorans who had entered the United States illegally. Her action and sentencing symbolizes the growing conflict between the Administration and church groups who support the sanctuary movement. Representatives of the sanctuary movement deny that their efforts are motivated politically to undermine governmental policy in Central America. "Members of many established churches say, however, that their efforts are humanitarian acts to protect people from persecution, torture and death in their homelands."[27] *The New York Times* sources indicate that more than one hundred congregations are supporting this venture. The support of such church figures as Bishop John J. Fitzpatrick of the Diocese of Brownsville, Texas, has caused the Administration to act with caution. A diocesan representative stated to the *New York Times* interviewer: "We do not feel we are breaking any laws. Service to refugees is something the Church has done since its inception. We have no choice but to assist them for humanitarian reasons."[28]

The sanctuary movement is defended as more than humanitarian aid—and certainly more than a publicity stunt, as charged by the U.S. Immigration and Naturalization Service. Eric Jorstad has urged that "it is a challenge to the church to re-examine its self-understanding as the one, holy, catholic, and apostolic people of God . . . and poses a fundamental question to the northern Church: Is our practice in accord with our basic mission?"[29] To Jorstad, sanctuary represents the church's ultimate allegiance to God alone and calls the church to be truly one. Further, as refugees tell their story, a bond of solidarity is forged between Christians of North American and Central American countries. The sanctuary movement asks North American Christians "not only to be benefactors of the refugees, but also to be beneficiaries of their witness of faith."[30]

One characteristic that separates North American pastor-prophets from their brothers and sisters in Central America and South America is that their faithful stand does not immediately incur the possibility of physical harm, let alone death. But these are the risks faced by pastors in Central America. Marco Tulio Maruffo was an Italian priest working in Guatemala. While he was driving with a friend in a northeast region of the country, on July 2, 1981, a band of submachine gunners opened fire on the car and killed Maruffo. He was the ninth Catholic priest to be assassinated in Guatemala in twelve months. Columnist William Bedell cited the *Los Angeles Times* of April 13, 1981, which quoted an unnamed priest in El Salvador: "When I started doing this kind of work myself, I was told by the local National Guard commander, 'Look, Father, you're training leaders—and we can't allow that.' "[31] North Americans know all too well, by now, that one may lose one's life ministering in the troubled countries of Central America and South America merely because one is a member of a Christian community that speaks for the poor and the disenfranchised.

One should remember, however, that the Hebrew prophets' attention was turned inward, not outward, to keep the community true to those events that called it to be a comforting community. As God confronted and redeemed the people of Israel, they were called to act in comforting and redemptive ways toward one another and toward other nations. The prophets called Israel to be a people whose service to God would be expressed in the care of the weak and the helpless. This ministry of compassion was present in Jesus' relationship with people, often to people whose dignity had been stripped by society. One of the marks of the church is that it is to be a community whose members express that sense of care in their relationships with one another.

In turn, the church—in part at least—is to be present in society as a prophetic sign. Stanley Hauerwas proposes that the kind of comfort Christian people give and receive is integral to the church's identity as an ongoing interpretive community (e.g., Matthew 5:16). The church is called to be a sign of the kind of world we live in and of the kind of world it may become. The prophet must confront the uncaring society as one who is a member of a caring community. Such a church does not spawn prophets—as if the prophetic ministry is an individual effort. It is of the church's identity that it *is* prophetic, its presence an earnest of a redeemed creation. In a world in which governments, businesses, and communities often fail to nurture and care for the people toward whom they bear responsibilities (e.g., citizens, consumers), the kind of comfort that characterizes the nature of the church stands as a prophetic word. Further, the quality of that care is continually under judgment.

Not surprisingly, the church's record of prophetic pastoral ministry is uneven. It may be remembered that some of the harshest words recorded in the Gospels are spoken by Jesus, who warned his followers first to count the cost of doing so and to be aware of the consequences of setting out on the road, only to turn back. Christians are often cautious and hesitant, bearing muted witness to new life and being content to function as part of a system that has institutionalized inequality and poverty. We do not always hear the unambiguous summons of a righteous God to assume the prophetic office and champion the cause of the dispossessed. Yet when the people of God fail to act prophetically, the world is not left without a witness. The Hebrew scriptures bear witness to those occasions in the life of Israel when God raised up figures from outside the community to achieve the divine saving purpose for Israel. It was a Persian king whose support of Nehemiah enabled the prophet to rebuild Jerusalem. It was a Roman centurion whose request of Peter led to the opening of the apostles' eyes to the incorporation of the gentiles within God's purpose.

Perhaps one of the more significant characteristics of the prophet, and one that may help to distinguish "true" from "false" prophets, is that the prophet—and therefore the pro-

18

phetic community—cannot remain comfortable in an unjust society. Thus, the comforting ministry of a community, one characteristic of which is its pastoral task, can be fully exercised only when and if the underlying causes of discomfort are exposed and challenged. An event occurred in Pittsburgh on Easter Sunday, 1984, that deserved wider public attention in the church than it received initially. Twenty-five protestors loudly took over the morning worship service at Shadyside Presbyterian Church to draw attention to what they charged was a lack of action to redress the injuries suffered by thousands of unemployed steelworkers and their families. The protest, led by approximately thirty clergy and union members, had begun in October 1983 and was directed initially against Pittsburgh-area banks. Dead fish were forced into the overnight safe of one bank late on Friday evening. The resulting offensive odor prevented the bank from opening on Monday. (We are tempted to draw a parallel with Isaiah walking barefoot and naked in Jerusalem, or Jeremiah struggling under an ox yoke.) The union dissidents created a brief stir, but their action was resented and rejected in the Pittsburgh community.

On Easter Sunday, 1984, they adopted a different tactic, interrupting the morning service in an affluent suburb of Pittsburgh with a series of demands. They urged church members to "pressure their neighbors—the corporate leaders—into changing their investment policies and creating jobs."[32]

A clergyman who has played a key role in organizing the protest defended the Easter action as "a prophetic ministry. . . . We put the heat on to say, 'We can't put people in the streets.' To discard people is not scriptural."[33] But the group's "hard-ball" tactics alienated members of the affected congregations, as well as the union management, which rejected the group's methods. One of the congregations visited by the dissident group was East Liberty Presbyterian Church. On the Sunday after Easter, the pastor, Dr. Robert Hewett, invited protestors to address the congregation after the benediction. This was the first of three meetings and marked the first effort of the two parties—church and protesters—to listen to each other.

Hewett, reflecting on the incident, stated: "Regardless of the street theater involved, the church sought to be the church by showing empathy and compassion for the suffering of the unemployed."[34] He described how one union member, a member of a Christian congregation and the father of two children, shared with the East Liberty congregation the difficulty he faced as a Christian who felt the protesters were justified in drawing the attention of other Christians to their plight. He stressed that the union dissidents hoped that the congregations would stir the church on behalf of the jobless to mediate between the steelworkers and the corporate structures.

Of course, the plight of the jobless workers already was known to church members through the media or, more directly, in those instances in which members were employed by steel companies. The challenge presented by the union members was whether congregations or judicatories can or should assume any responsibility to speak to the conditions that had contributed to the rate of unemployment in the steel industry and, in particular, to the plight of families in Pennsylvania's Monongahela Valley. These conditions include the investment policies of large banks, the steel industry's management policies, and so forth. Hewett viewed the worker-church confrontation as "a significant challenge to the church," which must be open to the truth, *no matter from which source it may come.*"[35] With respect to the unionists' interruption of church worship and the dissident nature of the group that sponsored this action, they should be evaluated not on the basis of that source, but on the basis of the message they proclaimed, he added.

That the unorthodox means used by the protesters alienated many people in the community is clear. But it is

20

equally clear that they succeeded in awakening the consciences of congregations' members to pursue actions designed to address their plight. We again draw attention to the prophets' symbolic actions when customary levels of communication of concern appear to have failed. In Pittsburgh, church judicatories were challenged to examine what they could do to address both the immediate humanitarian issue and the complex question of reconciliation between union dissidents and management, through the church's roles as mediator and reconciler. The *Los Angeles Times* quoted Eberhard Von Waldow, professor of Old Testament at Pittsburgh Seminary: "I have a lot of sympathy for these young ministers in the Mon Valley. . . . They are trying to take their faith in Jesus Christ seriously. They feel the biblical message has to be proclaimed in a concrete situation." But, notes the article, Von Waldow reminded the clergy supporters of the workers that their activist approach precluded dialogue. "They are simply joining the traditional American labor-management confrontation." Still, Von Waldow blamed the pastors of the affluent congregations for not sufficiently challenging their members "with the message of biblical and social justice and the dignity of man. The church should be the forum for bringing opponents together—the suffering blue-collar worker and the executive who makes decisions."[36]

The protesters' actions constituted a word addressed to the church from outside its membership, calling the people of God to examine their nature and calling and their responsibility to the larger society. The response, at least in some congregations, has been to recognize that the church's ministry must integrate two concerns: (1) the pastoral response of care and compassion and (2) openness to questions of social justice raised by the dispossessed and disenfranchised. To labor assiduously to express care for those who suffer will be insufficient if such action masks a failure to address the underlying causes of their suffering. Prophetic pastoral ministry consists not of two types of actions, but of the one ministry,

21

offered in the name of the risen Lord who dispatched his laborers to the lanes and streets and highways.

There is a sense in which the prophetic function can be a two-edged sword. If the people of God, who are called on to speak prophetically on behalf of the poor against injustice, including economic and political injustice, fail to fulfill that ministry, there is ample evidence that prophetic voices will be raised from outside God's people. In the illustration from the Mon Valley, those voices were heard in the lament of desperate, jobless union members. For Australian churches, the voice was that of a newspaper columnist. Geoffrey Barker, reflecting on the relationship of the churches to the ruling political party—in this instance, the Australian Labor Party—suggested that the prime minister could ignore the role of the church only at his peril. He noted that "it is one of the paradoxes of [the Australian] secular society that Anglican church leaders can still apply great pressure, and attract wide support, when they decide to come out fighting on a social issue."[37] The specific issue that had attracted Barker's attention was an open letter from an Anglican archdeacon to Prime Minister Hawke on the nature and extent of poverty in Australia. "If the [Anglican] initiative is a sign that the church is lifting its game on the issue of poverty, then the Federal Government had better start looking to an adequate response."

Citing attempts to influence previous conservative governments that had met with little success, Barker challenged the church's leaders to adopt "another braver and riskier course. . . . Having demonstrated 12 years ago their ability to get a poverty inquiry (from a previous Labor government), they might now encourage (or pressure) this government to get on with its proposed inquiry into the distribution of wealth." But, he continued,

> It would certainly be much harder for the clergy of the established conservative church to sell this proposition to its middle class constituency. It is easier to say "fight poverty" than "in-

vestigate wealth." But such action is a necessary prerequisite to any effective expansion of the sort of distributive justice to which a Labor Government ought to be committed on behalf of the poor. *Regrettably, I suspect that this sort of proposal is unlikely to appeal to canons and archbishops. It is more likely to come from secular sources and the more radical arm of the old rugged cross.*[38]

Such a statement is indeed a prophetic challenge that the church cannot, in conscience, ignore, for the prophet cannot pick and choose among the causes that she or he opts to champion. Thus, in addition to a caring heart and a call for peace based on justice, a third characteristic of the "true" prophet is a single-minded integrity that unmasks and confronts untruth and deceit in whatever form they are encountered. The prophets knew that this is not an easy path to follow, a viewpoint echoed in the essays that follow.

The contributors to this book address the prophetic tasks of pastoral ministry from the standpoints of their respective disciplines. Stanley Hauerwas "skeptically" initiates the inquiry by characterizing the notion of "pastor as prophet" as "an improbable mission," improbable because of a perception that the prophetic and caring tasks of pastors seem contradictory. He sets the prophetic message in the context of societal, rather than individualistic, concerns. The essential role of the prophet, for Hauerwas, is to point to creation as the arena of God's providential care. In the Christian era, the role of the lone prophet, speaking for the community and challenging that community, becomes a communal function, a theme that is emphasized repeatedly by the contributors. That is, it is the community itself that is prophetic. In particular, pastoral ministry cannot help but serve the church's prophetic mission. Thus, for Hauerwas, it is not a question of pastor *or* prophet, but of how one ministers in the name of Jesus.

Walter Brueggemann's Old Testament perspective calls attention to the sovereign will of God, who creates community and whose passion and love for God's creation find voice in

23

the prophets. Brueggemann argues that prophetic ministry by nature is destabilizing in that it proclaims an alternative truth about the rule of God to that offered by a system corrupted by a selfish use of power by those who gained privilege at the expense of the poor. For Brueggemann, the prophetic question is properly, Who has the power for life—God, whose invitation to life will not be contained by our vested interests, or those who have the forms of power, but whose monopolies are ultimately broken on the anvil of truth and righteous living? Brueggemann turns to the figure of Elijah to underscore his message that to dichotomize pastoral and prophetic ministry is to misunderstand both. He concludes that pastoral ministry requires intentionality that is rigorous and prophetic.

The prophetic character of the ministry of Jesus discernible from the Gospel narratives is discussed by John Howard Yoder. Understanding that prophetism entails convictions that God cares about and intervenes in human history, Yoder asks how Jesus' understanding of God's intentions for the world was different from that of other prophets. The difference is found for Yoder not only in the substance of Jesus' prophetic vision, but also in the mode of its realization, that is, the way of the cross, not pietism or Zealot compulsion. Yoder sees Jesus' prophetic ministry as analogous to Moses' in that both sustained a people at the start of a new moment in history; it was different from Moses' in that in Jesus, God's intention for human history was instanced and defined. Yoder's final comments focus on the relevance of Jesus' prophetic ministry for the prophetic task of the whole people of God today.

Paul's understanding of the prophet and the prophetic role is described by George MacRae. Cautioning that Paul's primary self-understanding was that of an apostle, MacRae finds one instance in which Paul claims for himself a prophetic calling (Galatians 1:15). The function of an apostle, according to Paul, is to preach the gospel and establish churches. The prophetic task is to proclaim or interpret the will of God to humanity, a task not inconsistent with that of the apostle. MacRae examines early Christian understandings of prophets in order to set Paul's views in perspective. For Paul, a prophet simply is one who has the gift of prophecy. He or she speaks for God and for the edification of the community. As such, MacRae sees Paul's understandings of prophet and spiritual leader as identical in the sense that both interpret the will of God for situations not addressed by Jesus. Two major conclusions for contemporary ministry are drawn: (1) Interpreting the will of God for the present time is an essential part of ministry, even though there are dangers to doing so. (2) The focus of prophetic ministry is communal, even though the importance of the individual is not overlooked.

Daniel Migliore approaches the nature of prophetic ministry by considering two meanings of the term "the passion of God." He identifies God's partisanship for the poor and advocacy of justice for the dispossessed as a *prophetic,* and the Deity's suffering love for the afflicted as a *pastoral,* understanding of the passion of God. Migliore contends that the two are interdependent, certainly not mutually exclusive. The biblical witness, according to Migliore, compels us to hold them together and to let each correct and enrich the other.

This argument is developed by a study of the apathy of our culture that leads Migliore to conclude that God struggles against our apathy-producing idols of power, summoning us to pastoral compassion and to prophetic resistance. On this basis, he explores the pastoral task of prophetic ministry and the prophetic task of pastoral ministry. He develops a picture of our present apathy as a failure either to care deeply about other people or to take risks to oppose every form of human bondage. In the face of human care-lessness, the biblical witness presents a God who is the supremely passionate advocate of justice and whose power is defined precisely by the freedom to undergo passion for others.

A failure to hold the prophetic and pastoral ministries in unity results either in compassionless prophetic activism or in sentimental care-taking that lacks prophetic vision and commitment. The alternative is a ministry that reflects the passion of God through either a prophetic witness that is pastoral in intent or, to put the same image another way, a pastoral ministry that not only attacks abuse of power, but also finds expression in Christian community and discipleship.

The collection concludes with an essay by Jorge Lara-Braud that predates the papal rebuke on liberation theology. The essay traces the development of liberation theology in Central America and South America, highlighting its prophetic components. From the perspective of liberation theology, Lara-Braud states that when liberation and oppression are examined as polarities, they are seen to fall within a biblical perspective in which God acts in concrete historical situations to redeem and emancipate. Such a caring and gracious God always begins with the disenfranchised and the dispossessed, that is, the poor. The essential ministry of the South American churches to the church at large, according to Lara-Braud, is the prophetic nature of its pastoral ministry to the poor. The pastoral task of the church, as lived out in Central America and South America, is its prophetic defense of the right of the poor to live in a just social order, which may very well be through the creation of a renewed society in which all members are free from the bondage of sin.

These essays indicate that the prophetic has been and continues to be a key aspect of the ministry of God's people, revealing God's purpose for and to those within and apart from the community of faith. Each author contributes to an enriched understanding of the prophetic task, both past and present. But within the varied descriptions provided by the contributors, two themes recur: (1) There is an essential interdependence between prophetic and pastoral ministries, and (2) while there is a tendency to focus on individual prophets, the prophetic witness falls properly to the congregation as a whole. This book focuses on the prophetic dimension of pastoral ministry. As such, it addresses an almost neglected emphasis within contemporary literature on pastoral theology and the practice of pastoral ministry.

CHAPTER 2

The Pastor as Prophet: Ethical Reflections on an Improbable Mission

Stanley M. Hauerwas

Being a pastor and being a prophet are roles most assume cannot be easily reconciled. Indeed, many claim you cannot be both. Some pastors, such as Martin Luther King Jr., may be prophetic, but most pastors have to carry on the day-to-day tasks of ministry that are anything but prophetic. The sick must be visited, the couple seeking divorce must be counseled, and the staff-parish relations committee meeting must be attended. The problem, moreover, is not that such activities leave little time for being prophetic, but if one tries to be prophetic, the caring function of the pastoral tasks proves impossible. For the moral outrage that fuels the fires of a prophetic calling seems incompatible with the kind of openness necessary to being a caring pastor.

For example, consider Amos' message to the rich matrons of Samaria, in Amos 4:1–2:

Stanley M. Hauerwas, Ph.D., is professor of theological ethics at the Divinity School of Duke University, Durham, North Carolina.

27

> Hear this word, you cows of Bashan,
>> who are in the mountain of Samaria,
>> who oppress the poor, who crush the needy,
>> who say to their husbands, "Bring, that
>>> we may drink!"
>
> The Lord God has sworn by his holiness
>> that, behold, the days are coming upon you,
>> when they shall take you away with hooks.

Generally, it is not the best pastoral practice to approach the women of one's congregation with the appellation "cows of Bashan." Moreover, Amos' depiction of these well-to-do women who have turned their husbands into servants is unrelenting. It is so because he draws a direct connection between their lives of luxury and the injustice perpetrated on the poor. He does not even try to help them see that there might be other possibilities that could make their lives more fulfilling, but instead delivers an uncompromising message of destruction. This kind of prophetic role simply does not seem compatible with the best insights of clinical pastoral education methodology. After all, Amos should have realized that these "cows" are also people in pain who deserve the same kind of care that he thinks should be directed toward the poor. If we are to minister to the "cows of Bashan," it seems that Amos' rhetoric, as well as his practice, will have to change.

The problem of being a prophetic pastor is particularly compounded by the cultural situation of the church. The church exists and must find a way to sustain itself in a buyer's market. The church no longer represents a community of authority through which the minister exercises leadership by calling the community to live in accordance with its own best convictions. Rather, the church has become a voluntary institution in which membership is determined by the consent of the individual believer. As Joseph Hough has observed in such a situation, the authority of the religious leader is increasingly based "not on his or her ability to interpret a body of authoritative teaching, but on the ability to persuade religiously inclined persons of at least the importance of, if not the superiority of, his/her own teaching."[1]

Indeed, that way of putting the matter is almost too optimistic, as membership in a church and loyalty to a pastor are seldom determined by a sense of the importance of the pastor's teaching. More important is whether the pastor has a winning personality. Such a situation is not conducive to encouraging pastors to take up a prophetic role. The congregation may put up with the pastor being concerned with social issues, such as U.S. nuclear policy, but they will hardly put up with the pastor turning the same kind of critical scrutiny toward his or her own congregation. We are all like the old woman who "Amened" her pastor when he preached against drinking, cursing, and philandering but when he criticized the use of snuff said, "Preacher, you've done stopped preaching and started to meddle."

Yet I think it is a mistake to assume that the inability of clergy to be prophetic is due solely to the necessity to please their constituency. As Reinhold Niebuhr suggested in his *Leaves from the Notebook of a Tamed Cynic,* the situation is much more complex. He says:

> I am not surprised that most prophets are itinerants. Critics of the church think we preachers are afraid to tell the truth because we are economically dependent upon the people of our church. There is something in that, but it does not quite get to the root of the matter. I certainly could easily enough get more money than I am securing now, and yet I catch myself weighing my words and gauging their possible effect upon this and that person. I think the real clue to the tameness of a preacher is the difficulty one finds in telling unpleasant truths to people whom one has learned to love. To speak the truth in love is a difficult, and sometimes an almost impossible, achievement. If you speak the truth unqualifiedly, that is usually because your ire has been aroused or because you have no personal attachment to the object of your strictures. Once personal contact is established you are very prone to temper your wind to the shorn sheep. It is certainly difficult to

be human and honest at the same time. I'm not surprised that most budding prophets are tamed in time to become harmless parish priests.[2]

Thus, Niebuhr observes that clergy cannot rush into a congregation that has been fed from its infancy on the individualistic ethic of Protestantism and that is immersed in a civilization in which individualism runs riot and expect to develop a social conscience among the people in two weeks. Nor do they have the right to insinuate that the church is full of hypocrites because the members do not see what they see.

> Of course it is not easy to speak the truth in love without losing a part of the truth, and therefore one ought not be too critical of those who put their emphasis on the truth rather than on love. But if a man is not willing to try, at least, to be pedagogical, and if in addition he suffers from a martyr complex, he has no place in the ministry. Undoubtedly there are more ministers who violate their conscience than such as suffer for conscience sake. But that is no reason why those who have a robust conscience should not try to master the pedagogical art.[3]

For as Niebuhr observes, "if the Christian adventure is made a mutual search for the truth in which the preacher is merely a leader among many searchers and is conscious of the same difficulties in his own experience which he notes in others, I do not see why he cannot be a prophet without being forced into itinerancy."[4] But one must observe that Niebuhr himself did not remain in the parish ministry.

It seems therefore that the improbability of the pastor as a prophet—or at least the same person being at once a prophet and pastor—manifests the classic tension between love and justice. Just to the extent we seek justice we often seem to have to do the unloving or at least harsh thing. The tension is, of course, an old one, although it has taken many different forms. It is sometimes depicted as that between the priest and the prophet; at other times it seems to be between realist and idealist. The kind of love and care that is necessary for the upbuilding of the community finally seems to be in tension with the demand that we be a people in critical judgment on our society. No easy resolution seems possible.

Yet I am not at all happy with this account of our situation. Indeed, I regard the current tension between those who would emphasize more the nurturing aspect of ministry and those who would stress the prophetic as disastrous both for∠ the training of ministers as well as for the practice of the ministry.[5] What we need is a recovery of how the pastoral tasks are fundamentally prophetic when they are appreciated as necessary for the upbuilding of a prophetic community. Because we lack the conceptual and sociological terms necessary to move such a claim beyond mere assertion, the attempt to make such a case is by no means easy. However, I hope at least to begin that process by developing an account of prophecy that will illumine the nature of ministry.

Before trying to develop my constructive suggestions, I think that it is important to challenge a certain picture of the ethical significance of the prophets. Ethicists have tended to underscore the tension I have tried to depict by downplaying the pastoral side of the ministry in favor of the prophetic. That they have done so is not surprising, as Christian ethics as a distinguishable discipline began in America among Protestants with a rediscovery of the ethical significance of the prophets. No one exemplifies this better than Walter Rauschenbusch, whose account of the prophets is well worth our attention. For Rauschenbusch's depiction of the prophets, particularly when assessing their ethical significance, continues to be widely shared even though his account in many ways distorts the nature of prophecy. These distortions help to explain why we continue to suffer from the assumption that when a minister becomes a prophet he or she becomes less a pastor.

Rauschenbusch on the Prophets

Rauschenbusch begins *Christianity and the Social Crisis* with an extended discussion of the prophets.[6] That he does so is not simply because he was trying for historical completeness, but because the prophets stood for everything he thought was right about Christianity. Indeed, for Rauschenbusch, it is not Jesus who completes the prophets, but rather Jesus is but the prophetic spirit rising from the dead. The rest of the Old Testament, therefore, can safely be ignored because the prophets "are the beating heart of the Old Testament. Modern study has shown that they were the real makers of the unique religious life of Israel. If all that proceeded from them, directly or indirectly, were eliminated from the Old Testament, there would be little left to appeal to the moral and religious judgment of the modern world."[7]

Rauschenbusch does not attempt to describe the work of the prophets in historical sequence. Rather, he tries to lay bare the large and permanent characteristics that are common to all prophets and that he assumes have lasting relevance. The first and most important of those characteristics is the prophetic insistence that right life is as important as true worship. "The prophets were the heralds of the fundamental truth that religion and ethics are inseparable, and that ethical conduct is the supreme and sufficient religious act."[8] They therefore challenged the "primitive religious" conviction that God is a tribal God concerned primarily with worship and controlling nature. Brushing aside sacrificial ritual, Hosea spoke for all the prophets by proclaiming that God desires "steadfast love and not sacrifice [Hos. 6:6]."[9]

But it is equally important to note that the morality that the prophets insist is central to our relation with God is not

> merely the private morality of the home, but the public morality on which national life is founded. They said less about the pure heart for the individual than of just institutions for the nation. The twin evils against which the prophet launched the

condemnation of Jehovah were injustice and oppression. The religious ideal of Israel was the theocracy. But the theocracy meant the complete penetration of the national life by religious morality. It meant politics in the name of God. That line by which we have tacitly separated the domain of public affairs and the domain of Christian life was unknown to them.[10]

The prophets were public men and their primary concerns were with public affairs. They were not religious individualists, but they thought of Israel and Judah as organic totalities. They thus anticipated our modern scientific comprehension of social development that rightly contends that society is more than a collection of individuals. Just as individuals can sin, so can whole societies, and it was with the latter that the prophets were uniquely concerned.

Moreover, the prophets' social concern, even for the most aristocratic among them, was entirely on the side of the poorer classes.

The edge of their invectives was turned against the land-hungry of the landed aristocracy who "joined house to house and laid field to field," till a country of sturdy peasants was turned into a series of great estates; against the capitalistic ruthlessness that "sold the righteous for silver and the needy for a pair of shoes," thrusting the poor free-man into slavery to collect a trifling debt; against the venality of the judges who took bribes and had a double standard of law for the rich and the poor. This dominant trait of their moral feeling reacted on their theology, so that it became one of the fundamental attributes of their God that he was the husband of the widow, the father of the orphan, and the protector of the stranger.[11]

According to Rauschenbusch, there were good historical reasons for the prophets to side with the poor. For

when the nomad tribes of Israel settled in Canaan and gradually became an agricultural people, they set out on their development toward civilization with ancient customs and rooted ideas that long protected primitive democracy and equality. It was the decay of the primitive democracy and the

33

growth of luxury, tyranny, extortion, of court life and a feudal nobility, which Samuel wisely feared when the people demanded a king.[12]

Thus, early Israel was much like the period in America's development when there was no social caste and a fair distribution of the means of production prevailed.

In fact, the rise of the prophets corresponded to the increase and unequal distribution of wealth in Israel. "The old democratic instinct of the people angrily resented this upstart tyranny."[13] Thus, Amos was the first of the great social prophets who not only uttered the message of God, but also expressed the feelings of the agrarian class. "The championship of the poor by the prophets was not due to the inflow of novel social ideals, but to the survival of nobler conceptions to which they clung in the face of distorted social conditions created by the new commercialism. They were the voice of an untainted popular conscience, made bold by religious faith."[14]

The prophets, however, were not only social reformers, but also called the nation to be true to itself. Consequently, the same national crisis that created the kingship also began the higher career of the prophets. Until that moment they had been mainly soothsayers whose predictions had not been based on any fundamental moral convictions. But now their patriotism was the emancipating power that allowed them to save the faith of the people amid the ruins of their national past.

> They asserted that Jehovah is fundamentally a god of righteousness, and a god of Israel only in so far as Israel was a nation of righteousness. God moves on the plane of universal and impartial ethical law. Assyria belongs to him as well as Israel. He would live and be just even if Israel was broken. Israel was not a pet child that would escape the rod. Its prerogative was the revelation of God's will and not any immunity from the penalties of the moral law. The relation of the nation to Jehovah was not a natural right and privilege, but rested on moral conditions.[15]

Owing to the breadth and inclusiveness of their religious sympathy, the prophets were able to discover the significance of individual piety. Thus, Jeremiah, amid the breakup of the nation, heard the

> insistent inner voice of God, and the consciousness of this personal communion with Jehovah was his stay and comfort. This was a wonderful triumph of religion, an evidence of the indestructibility of the religious impulse. It was fraught with far-reaching importance for the future of religion and of humanity in general. The subtlest springs of human personality were liberated when the individual realized that he personally was dear to God and could work out his salvation not as a member of his nation, but as a man by virtue of his humanity.[16]

This discovery of personal religion was never an end in itself, but rather a means to an end that was always social. Now the prophets sought to build a society that honored the dignity of the individual.

The gain that came with the discovery of personal religion brought with it a loss. The social vision became bleak in the exile, so rather than condemn sins of human beings against other humans, as the older prophets had done, Ezekiel dwelt on sins of human beings against God. Not justice, but holiness became fundamental, and the latter was understood primarily in terms of ceremonial correctness. Despite the prophetic character of Ezekiel's life, it is impossible, suggests Rauschenbusch, not to sense the beginning of religious decadence in Ezekiel's vision. "Religion had grown narrower and feebler when it was forced from the great national and human interests into an ecclesiastical attitude of mind."[17]

So runs Rauschenbusch's account of the ethical significance of the prophets. It is extremely instructive to us both for where he is correct and where in error. He is certainly right to emphasize the inner relation between ethics and religion as represented by the prophets. Moreover, he is right to emphasize the social character of the prophetic critique. Yet on the whole, his depiction of the prophets is decidedly one-sided.

To say that Rauschenbusch used the prophets to confirm a view of religion and ethics he had reached on other grounds is probably too strong, but the prophets still look far too much like what Rauschenbusch and his fellow "social-gospelers" had come to believe Christianity should be about.

This is not to say that Rauschenbusch ignored the best historical scholarship of his day concerning the prophets. On the contrary, his views were determined by the scholarly consensus that had developed in his time. That such is the case is but a reminder that the "scholarly consensus" is as open to ideological distortion as our own theology. Particularly destructive in the picture of the prophets that influenced Rauschenbusch is the inherent anti-Semitism that saw "Judaism" as the "decline" from the great heights of prophetic insight.[18]

For our purposes, at least two important lessons need to be drawn from Rauschenbusch's portrayal of the prophets. First, we should be suspicious of characterizations of prophecy that fail to appreciate the rich diversity of prophecy. If we have learned anything about the prophets since Rauschenbusch's time it is that prophetism was an extraordinarily varied phenomenon in Israel that served different purposes at different times. The prophets by no means spoke with a single voice, nor did they share the same set of theological presuppositions. Some of them, as Rauschenbusch suggests, seem to have identified more with the exodus traditions in a manner that put them in tension with the development of the kingship, whereas others drew on the Davidic covenant as central to Israel's identity. As Joseph Blenkinsopp has suggested, in the early centuries, and to a limited extent in the later period, prophecy was connected with warfare and cult,[19] but such a generalization is not sufficient to characterize all prophetic activity. It does, however, help us to appreciate how extraordinary it was that Amos later suggested that Israel's warrior God had now declared war on his own people.[20]

What must be guarded against is finding in the prophets a confirmation of a peculiar theological or ethical insight that one thinks particularly important for the current religious situation. This is not to say that the prophetic literature may not have significant contributions to make that challenge some of one's set assumptions, but one cannot assume that the current understanding of the "prophetic" is in fact synonymous with the role of the prophets of the Hebrew scriptures. For example, the prophets are often treated as social radicals who were willing to overthrow their social order in the interest of justice. Yet one is increasingly aware that many of the prophets were profound social conservatives who were seeking not to overthrow the status quo, but to maintain it, or even to return to a prior way of life.

It is important, second, to challenge Rauschenbusch's account of the prophets primarily as ethical reformers. No doubt Gerhard von Rad's stress on the centrality of the "word of God" to characterize prophetic activity may reflect more an influence of Karl Barth than an accurate account of prophecy, yet von Rad is surely right when he says that the prophets cannot be properly understood simply as moral reformers.[21] One cannot easily overlook the ecstatic and seer-like aspects of the prophets, as Rauschenbusch tries to do. Even as cautious a historian as Blenkinsopp suggests:

> The standard introductory formula "Thus says Yahweh" is taken from the established protocol of official messages and letters in the ancient Near East, pointing to the prophetic self-designation as emissary of Yahweh. The conviction of acting under such a mandate is essential to understanding how the prophets thought of their authority and role in society, and can therefore provide a starting point for addressing the central issue of prophetic identity.[22]

Rauschenbusch's characterization of the prophets primarily as ethical reformers, therefore, cannot be sustained. Or, more accurately, Rauschenbusch is right to emphasize the centrality of ethics for characterizing the activity of the prophets, but his account of ethics is far too limited. This is understandable, given the extraordinary social injustices of his own day (I

37

am not convinced that we face any less injustice in our day; we just fail to see it because we are less imaginative than Rauschenbusch and his friends). Yet when "ethics" is understood primarily as a call for justice against the status quo, we overlook those presuppositions that are necessary to sustain such an endeavor, for the question of what kind of community is necessary to sustain the task of so interpreting the world is ignored. Therefore, I have provided an account of prophecy that not only does greater justice to the full range of prophetic activity as exhibited in the scripture, but also helps us to better understand the prophetic nature of the pastoral office.

The Prophetic Nature of the Pastoral Office:
A Theological Proposal

I want to make clear certain methodological presuppositions about the account of prophecy I have tried to develop. First and foremost, the account of prophecy is a theological proposal that does not attempt to be faithful in every aspect of prophetic activity as we find it displayed in the Hebrew scriptures. Certainly, any constructive theological proposal about prophecy will be accountable to scripture, but any account or understanding of the nature and continuing significance of prophecy for the church cannot simply be an attempt to mimic the prophets of Israel.

One of the most significant reasons that our understanding of prophecy cannot help but be a theological proposal is that for Christians no account of prophecy can be divorced from Christological considerations. This is not just because Jesus in many ways is best understood, both historically and theologically, as a prophet, but also because his work has made a decisive difference in how Christians are to understand their prophetic role. Because Jesus was who he was, Christians cannot help but be prophetic, since now their very existence is a prophetic sign of God's refusal to abandon creation. If the essential role of the prophet is to interpret the world in terms

38

of God's providential care, then the church's very existence is prophetic, for without the church we could not know who we are or in what kind of world we exist.

John Howard Yoder has suggested that the significance of the prophets can only be appreciated if we understand that Israel was constituted and existed as a people only as they gathered around events that were continually commemorated. Therefore, the prophet was uniquely important to Israel's existence because the prophet was the one who interpreted past, present, and future in the light of God's calling of Israel.

> It was he who spoke to what was going on in history and said what it means. The priest interprets nature. He speaks to what is always the same and what happens again every year. The priest manages the interpretation of the circles of the stars and the crops and flocks. He is dealing with stability—with that which is routine and recurrent. The prophet interprets events which happen but once, or if he sees pattern in the events it is a meaningful, directional, pattern. Speaking culturally, descriptively and sociologically the scholars all have to agree that Israel is the type of people that gathered around the meaning of certain events and looked in the direction which the prophets said those events were leading. We could say it as well theologically. The concept of the *word of the Lord* has in Hebrew thought a unique objective quality. The prophet is simply a channel for this word. It is spoken through him. Often, usually, it is spoken with his personal involvement. He says something he agrees with, believes and understands and cares about. But sometimes actually it is said without his personal involvement. There are times when he does not know what he is saying, or does not know what it means, or does not like it. The prophet cannot call back the word, he cannot guide it. The word is almost personalized. It goes out and it does its work. It was the word of Jahweh spoken through the prophets which make Israel Israel.[23]

This interpretation of the prophetic office is confirmed by Blenkinsopp's discussion of the profound and widespread transformation of prophecy after the loss of national independence and royal patronage.

Increasingly reference to former prophets, occasional laments of the absence of prophetic guidance and, not least, the well-attested practice of adapting earlier prophetic sayings to new situations (e.g., in Zech. 1—8) are symptomatic of this new situation. With the availability of prophetic material in writing, the emphasis was less on direct inspired utterance and more on the inspired interpretation of past prophecy. Correspondingly, there was an increasing sense that, in the normal course of events, God does not communicate directly but has revealed his will and purpose in past communications whose bearing on the present situation remains to be elucidated.[24]

So, the prophet remains interpreter, but now the history of the prophetic activity becomes the means of interpretation. Blenkinsopp notes that this extremely important shift was decisive for the self-understanding of the community that began to preserve the prophetic texts. For since the text can be interpreted in more than one way, the control of this function was also a political factor in the disposal of power within the community. As Blenkinsopp suggests, "the problem for those who preserved these texts and took them seriously was: How can the word of God addressed to our ancestors who lived in a different age and faced different problems become a word of God for us today?"[25] Prophecy is no longer relegated to individuals, but now becomes a task of the whole community as the community seeks to discern and interpret events in the light of God's past relation with them.

It is against this background that one asks in what sense was Jesus a prophet. Jesus was a prophet not only because he spoke the words of God for God, but also because in him the revealed and the revealer are one. That is, Jesus not only reveals the words of God, but his person is God's revelation as well. Moreover, it is his person that now makes possible the decisive interpretation of the world that demands the existence of a different kind of community. In fact, it is a commu-

40

nity of interpretation that is based on the profound claim in 1 John 1: 2 that he "was made manifest" not only through his words, but also in his person. "'In many and various ways God spoke of old to our fathers by the prophets, but in these last days he has spoken to us by a son.' Not by the *words* of a son, but the being, the presence of his son. So Jesus in his person is a new kind of communication or manifesting or revealing which goes beyond what words can do."[26]

Jesus does not make irrelevant all past prophecy, nor does he render future prophecy irrelevant, but rather he now becomes the standard by which the past is understood and the future right anticipated. We still have much to learn and we will continue to need prophetic figures to challenge us to see that God will often call us in unanticipated ways to be God's faithful people. Indeed, it is because of the life of this man, Jesus, that the community formed by his memory can live open to the unanticipated—open to that which may challenge it to rethink those interpretations of its past. Such a community can be open to the new, which is as common as the birth of a child, because it is sustained by the remembering that for all time God has made it safe through the life, death, and resurrection of Jesus of Nazareth.[27]

For such a community, prophecy is no longer solely the role of specific individuals, although individual prophets will, I hope, still be present. It is the community itself that is now prophetic, for it is a community formed by the life and death of Jesus of Nazareth, which means that it cannot be what it is without understanding itself to be accountable to the great prophets of Israel. Just to the extent that it holds itself so accountable by its very existence it becomes a prophetic community as it carries in its very being the symbols that help the church to understand what it is and what kind of world it exists in. The church is prophetic, because without it, the world would have no means of knowing that it is the world; that is, the world is without a history sufficient to understand itself as God's creation.

41

To stress the interpretative role of the prophet does not exclude the critical dimension of the prophetic task. The prophet still must deliver the word of judgment. The prophet still must challenge those who think that their power can make their nation safe. The prophet cannot avoid challenging the injustice that is all the more powerful because we have learned to accept it as part of the landscape. That the prophet performs such tasks, however, is but an aspect of the calling to keep the community true to the story that determines its character as the church of Jesus of Nazareth.

This is why the prophetic task is at once so conservative and yet radical. Prophecy is meant to keep us true to the One who has made and continues to make us what we are. Just as Israel's prophets insisted that Israel be the kind of community that made it possible to remember its past, so the church must be the kind of community capable of telling the story of a crucified messiah. The task is, therefore, conservative, but the means are decidedly radical, for the very content of the story requires us to be willing to face our sinfulness as a people who constantly try to avoid the truth about ourselves and our world. As we are told in 1 John 2:9–11, we cannot say that we are in the light, that we are followers of Jesus the Christ, yet hate our brother or our sister. "He who says he is in the light and hates his brother is in the darkness still. He who loves his brother abides in the light, and in it there is no cause for stumbling. But he who hates his brother is in the darkness and walks in the darkness, and does not know where he is going, because the darkness has blinded his eyes."

The problem, therefore, with accounts such as that of Rauschenbusch, that stress the prophets' ethical significance, is not that the prophetic task does not involve ethics. Rather, the problem is with the kind of ethics that is entailed. For the ethical is not limited to questions of justice, but involves the question of interpretation in light of the truth we are convinced has been revealed through the life, death, and resurrection of Jesus. To be such an interpretative community means that we must be a people transformed by that story. It is not simply a question of just actions and institutions; rather, we must be people who are capable of loving the stranger. This is why the subject of prophetic activity is, first of all, the community itself, not those who are not of the community.

But what does all this have to do with understanding the prophetic nature of pastoral office? First, and most important, it means that in being prophetic the pastor stands in and for the community. It is the pastor's task to hold before the community the story that determines its existence and makes it possible, not for the pastor to be prophetic, but for the community to fulfill its calling as God's own. The pastoral task is prophetic, just as the means that are peculiar to the church's ministry help to remind the community of the story that makes that community prophetic. There can be no more prophetic task than the preaching of the word and the serving of the eucharist, for it is through them that the church is constituted as God's people in a world that does not know God. So, it is not a question of whether the pastor can be prophetic, but rather that the pastor *must* be prophetic, given the nature of the community that he or she serves.

Moreover, from this perspective, there can be in principle no conflict between the "pastoral tasks" and the prophetic. Visiting the sick may appear to be mundane, but it is no less a prophetic task than protesting against the idolatry of the nation state. Indeed, it is, in a sense, part of the protest against such idolatry, as it is one of the ways the church makes clear its refusal to let the state or wider society determine who it will and will not serve. Thus, those who insist on caring for the persecuted, even if such care requires us to ignore national boundaries, are acting pastorally and prophetically. Or again, taking the time to talk with a couple who are seeking a divorce may be prophetic if such counseling is informed by the church's prophetic commitment to faithfulness in a world almost devoid of any sense of constancy. The only question about whether such work can be prophetic is when such activities no longer draw on the story and habits that form the church, but instead underwrite our cultural assumptions about marriage and the care of the sick and the persecuted.

When "pastoral tasks" are undertaken as a means to help the church remember who it is as the church, they cannot help but serve the church's prophetic mission, for the body is built up as we learn to minister to one another in the name of Christ. The church does not provide comfort, but the comfort of Christ. The church does not give us peace, but the peace of Christ. Such comfort and such peace may be troubling indeed for both the church and the world, but it is no less comfort and peace for that.

The pastor, therefore, is engaged in a constant task of helping the church interpret itself and the world through the many small and great tasks that build up the people of God. It is not a question of pastor *or* prophet, but how one pastors. Pastoring will be authentic to the extent that it avoids the sentimentalities that abound today concerning what it means to be a "caring community." For the church is not just another haven in the storm to protect some from the ravages of modernity, but a people who care so deeply that they refuse to do anything else than speak the truth in love.[28]

Pastoral Counseling as Prophetic: An Example

Obviously, much more needs to be said to develop fully my account of the pastoral task as one of prophetic interpretation. In particular, much more would need to be said about the content of the story of Jesus that I have suggested forms the church's identity. But rather than developing my proposal in an abstract way, I have provided an example that I hope will suggest how clergy must be prophetic even in their day-to-day activities. I have purposely chosen an example from a counseling context, since so often it is in that area that it seems so difficult for the pastor to be prophetic. Another reason I have chosen such an example is because it is often claimed that in such pastoral situations it is hard to be rigorous in giving ethical advice.[29] Insofar as the prophetic is identified with the ethical, it thus seems no easy resolution can be effected between the pastoral task and the ethical.

During 1984, Methodism was in the throes of celebrating its bicentennial in the United States. In preparation for that event, a conference was held at Emory University, in Atlanta, Georgia, to assess Methodist theological strength for the next century. I was part of a seminar on the Methodist stress on perfection and virtue as continuing themes of church life. As some of us theorized about how sanctification might be understood in terms of the virtues, a young pastor told a story that he thought exhibited some of the difficulties of translating such theoretical emphases into practical terms.

He told of a young mother, a member of his church, who came to him considering the possibility of an abortion. She and her husband had two children, and they had recently decided to seek a divorce; or more accurately, the husband had decided that they should divorce and she had acquiesced. The husband was a rather reserved man, an engineer with an extremely good job and income. They lived in a community of other young professionals in which divorce was common. Although the reasons for the divorce were not clear, it was obviously a situation that had been building for some time.

The young pastor, who had great sympathy for the woman, at first found her ambivalent about whether she could or should have an abortion. She had moral reservations about abortion in general and was unsure whether or not she could live with the results. She received no support from her husband, who simply abandoned her in her decision-making, taking no responsibility for the outcome one way or the other. The pastor said that because he did not think it right to be moralistic about abortion, he simply tried to help her reach a decision that would be best for her and her children in light of

45

her prospective divorce. He therefore sent her to a professional counselor who would be better able to help her resolve her feelings.

Through her counseling sessions, she came to the conclusion that she would be better off having an abortion. The counselor had been particularly important because she felt supported by him. His acceptance of her seemed to give the necessary permission she needed to have the abortion. The pastor then arranged for her to have the abortion in an appropriate medical setting and continued to support her after the abortion.

Nothing about this story is unique. It is commonplace in the professional lives of many clergy. Yet I think it is a story of failure—failure of community and failure of the pastor. It was a failure, first, because the pastor was so afraid of being "moralistic" that he could not help the woman to see how her situation was related to or involved her Christian commitments. He failed to help her interpret her situation in light of her relation to the Christian community and that community's support of her.

Because he was afraid to place any more burden on this woman, he failed to help her perceive all that was happening or to call her to have greater confidence in herself. For example, I asked him if he had suggested to her that perhaps her anger at her husband for deciding to end the marriage was involved in her contemplation of abortion. He said that it had never even occurred to him. He was trying so hard to be understanding that in being nonjudgmental he had no way of drawing on the very resources of the gospel to inform his ministry to her. It had never occurred to him that the category of sin might be relevant to such situations. We cannot know in fact whether this young woman was seeking to kill her child as a means of attacking her husband—but what could be more human? God knows the terrible irony that, for many of us, our hates are more precious to us than even our self-esteem.

Moreover, by trying to understand, the pastor asked nothing from his community. He simply accepted the assumption that the people of his church would see this woman's situation as her problem—one that had no relation to them. As a result, abortion could not help but appear "the best for all concerned." The pastor did not consider calling on the church to be a community of people who care about one another so that they might even support one another to have children under less-than-happy circumstances. Therefore, he could not relate to this mother as an officer of a community formed by a story of presence and care; he had to relate to her as one anonymous person relating to another anonymous person in need. All he represented was a vague sense of serving a community that cares about people, but not enough of a community to provide the kind of moral and physical support that might make this woman's loneliness less burdensome.

If that is an example of pastoral care, then I think it is surely right that there is a tension between pastoral and prophetic. For such care in no way draws on or is informed by the convictions of a community pledged to care for the widow and the orphan, for the abandoned mother, or for the poor because of the kind of God that has called it into being. Such a community cannot help but produce pastors who acquiesce to the sentimentality of a culture that assumes the way to care for people is to try to make their lives less difficult. Moreover, such a community cannot help but end with a self-hating leadership who cannot avoid despair because they know the distance between what they are and what they should be.[30] Indeed, it may be that agony will prove to be prophetic as it becomes the means by which to secure a new sense of community. What could be of more prophetic significance for the church than for the ordained ministry to recover a sense of its integrity—that the pastor, even as counselor, is such a representative of Christ's people?

I do not mean to suggest that this pastor would have been prophetic if he had responded to the woman by condemning any idea of her having an abortion; we have all the self-righteousness we need in the church already.[31] Rather, I am suggesting that what is wrong with how he proceeded is that he did nothing through his counseling to remind the woman what it meant for her to be a Christian, or to remind his community what it would mean for them to be people of aid and help in such circumstances. As a result, this kind of care does nothing to help us better understand why we find ourselves in such situations. Moreover, too often the "solutions" only perpetuate the malady.

I know of no magic or easy solutions, but I do have faith in the prophetic nature of God's church. I do not believe that the church is without resources to reclaim its task of being God's presence in the world. Surely one of these resources is a faith that those who are called to the pastoral ministry will find the courage to challenge us to live up to our avowed commitments as Christians. Such a task will require nothing less than the willingness to trust our language to be a truthful account of the way we are and the way the world is. Such a trust may require that we Christians again look, as well as live, differently from most of our neighbors. We have no other choice if we are to be faithful to the prophetic task to which the Christian people are called.

CHAPTER 3

The Prophet as a
Destabilizing Presence

Walter Brueggemann

Both traditional conservatives and conventional liberals misunderstand the prophetic dimension of Israel's faith. The former, in my judgment, tend to make too much of the predictive element, as though the prophets are forecasting, with particular reference to Jesus. The latter tend to understand the prophets primarily in terms of social action and righteous indignation. Both misunderstandings have an element of truth. It is true, on the one hand, that the prophets do care about the future, and they do believe that in the future, God will bring the historical process to obedience. On the other hand, the prophets do care intensely about the moral shape of society, so they assault every social disorder. I have tried to articulate an alternative understanding of the prophets that reflects the current inclinations of scholarship[1]

Walter Brueggemann, Ph.D., is professor of Old Testament and evangelical professor of biblical interpretation at Eden Theological Seminary, Webster Groves, Missouri.

and that I hope is useful for the practice of pastoral ministry in our own context.

The Prophets

My impression is that the most helpful study of the prophets just now is an analysis of the social systems of ancient Israel that "construct reality" in various ways. That is, the prophets are not isolated individuals but can best be understood in terms of the organization of society and the performance of certain social roles.[2] Although the implications of what I have to say apply to the prophets generally, I take as my text the Elijah narrative. I am primarily concerned with the ways in which this narrative reflects, serves, and challenges social organization.

1. As the prophets understand it, society consists in *an organization of social power*. This may refer variously to land, money, hardware, technology.

2. The organization of social power is derived from and dependent on *the management, control, and articulation of social symbols* that, in our day, may be understood as access to the media. In that day, this process was largely managed and controlled by the temple community, which was the center of symbolic life. Thus, the priests held enormous power, perhaps analogous to the power of the media in our context.

3. The organization of *social power* and the administration of *social symbols* were intimately linked together. Each reinforces and legitimates the other. The two together constitute a *social system* that orders, defines, values, and legitimates all life. It seeks to contain and monopolize all social meanings and all social possibilities. It inclines to be effective at delivery of a "good life" for those who participate in and support the system. Such support is given through a variety of modes: political conformity, economic solidarity, ritual commonality,

50

epistemological assent, moral coherence. The system works well for all those who accept its definitions of reality.

The upshot of such a social achievement (which it is) is that *"the system is the solution"* for all social needs and hopes. Indeed, nothing of worth falls outside the system, so that the social system comes to be identified as being equivalent to reality. This is particularly evident in "creation theology," which speaks of "creation" but often seems to refer to a certain social system that is assigned ontological status as the embodiment of what the creator intended.[3] Both the managers and the benefactors of the system tend to absolutize the system, to preclude alternative notions of reality. Indeed, alternative notions of reality constitute a threat, for they assert that this way of organizing social power and social goods is not an absolute given, but only a historical contrivance. The goal of the managers and benefactors is to stabilize the system so that it is not noticed that it is a system, but there is only *reality*, the only possible, thinkable reality. And if no other social reality is thinkable or possible, then criticism of this one tends to be precluded. Thus, most participants in and benefactors of the system do not notice that it is a managed, contrived system to which there are alternatives. They notice only that there is a reality to be trusted, valued, and adhered to. The end result is that there is a kind of positivism that treats the social organization of power and symbols as an absolute given, "as it was in the beginning, is now and ever shall be." That system is deeply valued because it comes to its adherents as though the only alternative to this system is chaos, which is experienced practically as the loss of advantage.

Destabilizing Presence

The prophetic task in such a social world is to maintain a *destabilizing presence*, so that the system is not equated with reality, so that alternatives are thinkable, so that the absolute

51

claims of the system can be critiqued. Thus, the destabilizing effort of the prophets takes as its responsibility the attempt to counter the powerful forces of stabilization that are at work among the participants and benefactors of the social system.

One may identify a *ground* and an *impetus* for this vocation of destabilization. The ground for such destabilization is not that the prophets are simply "angry young men," filled with righteous indignation, who like to "go off" on people. The ground is that they have an alternative perception of social reality that they insist is true, and for which they want to create working space and allow for social possibility to emerge. That alternative perception of reality puts the presumed world of the regnant system in jeopardy. Such an alternative perception serves, by definition, to destabilize precisely when the alternative is stated or acted with clarity, so that the contrast is sharp. The contrast may be between the rule of God who liberates and the rule of idols that enslave, between the coming reign of God that invades and the present regime that sustains, between the yearning for justice and the experience of injustice. But note well, the prophetic is not understood primarily as denunciation or rejection, unless it is clear that there is a positive alternative available that, in fact, is true, gives life, and really functions.

The destabilization that results from such a powerful contrast may or may not be overt political action. On occasion, the prophets did speak directly about policy issues (perhaps most noticeably, Isaiah). But most often, the prophets issue a gesture or word that intends to play on the imagination of the community.[4] The preliminary point I want to make here is that prophecy is not in any overt, concrete sense political or social action. It is rather *an assault on public imagination,* aimed at showing that the present presumed world is not absolute, but that a thinkable alternative can be imagined, characterized, and lived in. The destabilization is, first of all, not revolutionary overthrow, but it is making available an alternative imagination that makes one aware that the presumed world is imagined, not given. Thus, the *prophetic* is an alternative to a *positivism* that is incapable of alternative, uneasy with critique, and so inclined to conformity.

The ground for such an alternative picture of reality is the sovereign rule of God. The prophets, skilled as they are with word pictures, relentlessly insist that the entire world must be imagined differently because of God's sovereignty.

Now it may seem to you that I have staked out a modest claim for the prophetic, that I have given away most of the great ideas for which "prophetic ministry" is embraced. My response is that first we need to look at what the poets of Israel do, and then we need to look at what is going on in our society. The truth is that because of the enormous fear in our social context, our government and its allies have constructed for us a fanciful world of fear, threat, security, and well-being that has little contact with the data at hand. But because we are managers and benefactors of the system, we find it easy and natural to accept this imagined world as real.

So the ground for prophetic destabilization is the alternative truth about the rule of God that gives the lie to our presumed worlds. The immediate *impetus* for much of the prophetic is the visible and daily presence of powerless and disenfranchised people. Robert Wilson, among others, has explored how this factor generates voices of destabilization. The socially critical point is that the social system that claims to be the solution is, in fact, a solution for some at the expense of others. As the system empowers and secures some, it renders powerless and marginalizes others. The ideological claim of the system is that it cares for all and provides for all. So the President can assert that a man losing his job in South Succotash is "not news." Or, the President's aide can say that he knows of no real data concerning hungry children. The system not only creates such disproportion, but then it also creates a set of lenses so that we look and genuinely do not see (Isaiah 6:9–10).

Israel's sense of the historical process is that the voices of the excluded cannot be silenced. They can be administered for a long time, but they will not be silenced. They can be administered for a long time, but they will not be finally nullified. They will cry out. And when they cry out, they constitute an attack on the system and in fact a delegitimation, for they assert that the system is not working, is not giving life, is not keeping its promises.

The prophets of the Old Testament discern a peculiar linkage between *the truth of God's rule* and *the voice of the marginal.* The former gives the long-term *ground;* the latter gives the immediate *impetus.* That ground of God's sure rule and the impetus of a voice of marginality constitute the alternative world of the prophets. When this is mobilized against the dominant imagination, it makes a powerful alternative. The prophets intend that the participants in the dominant system should hear enough to transform the system. But their characteristic experience is that assault on imagination only drives system people deeper into their closed imagination.[5] The helplessness of the prophets is that they cannot penetrate this dominant imagination when it is finally hardened. Then the question is simply whether that closed imagination can finally fend off the truth of God and the cry of neighbor. In every particular circumstance, this question is always quite open and yet to be decided.

The Elijah Narrative

Now with that general background, we may consider three episodes from the Elijah narrative. The Elijah narrative is a remarkable piece in 1 Kings (17—21), with accompanying pieces on Micaiah (1 Kings 22) and Elisha (2 Kings 1—10). These narratives form a distinct corpus in the literature of 1 and 2 Kings, clearly contrasted both to the usual royal formula and to the Deuteronomic editing, for there is almost no such marking on these texts. It is commonly presumed, as I do here, that these narratives are older than their royalhistorigraphic context.[6] It is likely that they were preserved and treasured in something of a folk culture and reflect such a community of storytelling. But I should also insist that the stories in their very character are not simply for entertainment, but in fact perform an important critical function. That is, the rather primitive quality of the narrative not only reflects a socially *primitive* community. It also reflects a socially *marginal* community that has kept its distance from the reason, language, and epistemology of the dominant culture. It has, I suggest, fashioned a reason, a language mode, and an epistemology resonant with its social, political, economic situation. These narratives, in their very mode, *enact marginality.* They perform an important social function, to state an alternative reality apart from the dominant reality. That social function is not created by placing these narratives in the context of the book of Kings but was the point of the narratives in their very first telling. The narratives are told, treasured, and practiced precisely in this community that wants to keep its freedom from the cultural perceptions of the royal system.

Now in saying this, I am urging that we read these texts with a kind of social responsiveness not honored by the historical-critical methods. Ask not what these texts *mean,* or even what they *say,* as though one may arrive at a conclusion and then summarize. Rather, ask what these texts *do,* in their inception and each time in their retelling. I argue that they propose to us an alternative world in which to live. They invite us to try it and for the moment to withdraw our intense allegiance to the world defined by the system. The stories have as their function to loosen our tight commitments to the life-world of our vested interests and for a moment to perceive the world differently.

The use of these stories by the Deuteronomic presentation of 1 and 2 Kings is complex. I have drawn the conclusion that the Deuteronomic editors were not fully contained in the royal world, but mount a massive critique against it.[7] One ground for that massive critique is precisely these stories that hold out an alternative. Thus, even the Deuteronomic historian may have understood that these narratives function to unmask and debunk the royal system. It may be for that reason that they occupy such a prominent place in the historical account.

One of the interesting questions for scholarship today is that these are prophetic *texts*.[8] Our usual way is to take the personality of the prophet as an example of what we are to do. So that we may consider how, in our situation, we may act like Elijah. There may be something in that. The problem that scholars now detect is that it is an appeal of *the example of a person* when in fact what we have is *the model of a text.* Current scholarship wants to argue that our role, insofar as these texts are concerned, is not that we should *replicate the person* of Elijah, but that we should *handle the text* so that it can have its say in the community.

The faith of the church is not vested in the person of Elijah. But it is staked very much on the claim of the text. So one will want to keep in mind that our tradition does not summon us to be prophets, but to let the prophetic text have its continued say among us. To let this text have its continued say is to let it be a continuing voice of destabilization in a tightly ordered system, for that was its primary and original function. So I consider with you three episodes in three texts that characterize three dimensions of prophetic destabilization.

Transformative Gestures of Solidarity

The first text, as model of prophetic destabilization, is in *1 Kings 17:9–24,* which I put under the rubric, "Transformative Gestures of Solidarity." The narrative falls into two parts, verses 9–16 and 17–24. It is introduced in a striking way with two significant elements:

(a) The word of the Lord came to him,
(b) "Arise, go to Zarephath, which belongs to Sidon, and dwell

there. Behold, I have commanded a widow there to feed
you."

Notice how abrupt and unaccommodating is the directive.
The narrator has no interest in accommodating the listening
community, in providing context or continuity. It is blurted
out in all its powerful discontinuity. The text is destabilizing in
its form because it offers a clean break. The initiative of the
story holds two things in juxtaposition. The entire action is by
the word. It is not explained but is under compulsion. There
is agency within the narrative that is not attributable to the
prophet. The word, however it is to be explained
phenomenonologically, is theologically presented as destabilizing. It breaks and it disorders life.

The second element is curious next to this awesome word.
Elijah is sent outside, outside his people, outside his normal
traffic pattern, outside the system. The *word* notices what lies
outside the *system*. Elijah is sent to the widow. He is sent
there to be fed by the widow. He is driven outside normal
support systems. He is not sent there with resources for her.
He is sent there to receive, to be given life precisely by this
one whom society has defined as having no life-resources. It is
not said that this is a testing of Elijah. But clearly, what the
sovereign word of Yahweh does is to drive the prophet out
beyond everything conventional and safe, perhaps to push
him to "faith alone."

The widow, by definition, is poor. "Widow" is a legal category for those without social power. She has no representative
in the village council, in the market, in the court. She is a
genuine "nobody," one whom the system is quite skillful in
discounting and nullifying. Yet Elijah is to be fed by her. The
story is remembered explicitly in Luke 4:26, where Jesus
talks about the reach of God beyond the social system. The
text seems to be strangely echoed in John 4, where Jesus
receives water from the unacceptable, disreputable woman at
the well.

So why tell the story? Well, likely it was told among widows and people like that. They did not regard themselves as without life-resources. The system thought so, but they knew better. Such communities at the margin do have strange ways in which to give life. By being sent there, Elijah is in an act of disengagement from the dominant support system. The story functions to assert, both in the community of the marginal and against the system, that the system does not have a monopoly on life. Elijah is sent to find life precisely outside the system.

This juxtaposition of *word* and *widow* is important for the prophetic. It is echoed in Isaiah 57:15:

> For thus says the high and lofty One
>   who inhabits eternity, whose name is Holy:
> I dwell in the high and holy place,
>   and also with him who is of a contrite and humble spirit,
> to revive the spirit of the humble,
>   and to revive the heart of the contrite.

The God of the word dwells on high. This God speaks and it is commanded. But this same one sojourns with the widow and all those outside the system. The word does not leave one at rest in a safe system, but drives one outside to the other place where God dwells.

So Elijah goes (v. 10). He is immediately obedient to the destabilizing word. We need to learn to read the text in terms of systems analysis. The imperative of Yahweh and the response of Elijah are a direct counter to the world view of the dominant system. This woman and all like her have been nullified. They do not exist. They are non-persons, invisible, without rights and without power. The social system does not notice or reckon with her. Probably King Ahab and his advisers had a government memo floating around showing that there really were no destitute widows. But the Word noticed. (If there is a sound of laughter lurking behind these words, it is because it is there!)

In this act of the commanding word and the responding

prophet, official reality is countered. These two together, lord and prophet, declare official reality to be a lie. The woman does exist. There really are widows. And in an odd way, they have social power that the regime cannot nullify. They can be a source of life.

So Elijah goes to her. She is gathering sticks (or picking greens) or whatever it is that marginal people do to stay alive on marginal land. And Elijah says, "Fetch me a little water" (cf. John 4:7). It is an incredible act of solidarity and certainly not do-good liberalism, for he undertakes no action on her behalf. He is present to her at the point of her possibility that officialdom had denied her. Then he ups the asking: "Give me bread." She pleads utter poverty. She had no bread, only a handful of meal, a little oil, and no prospect of any more. She knows she is to die. The system has fixed her fate in that way. Now read it as a systematically destabilizing narrative. It is an assertion that this is social reality in Israel. There really are people like this. They really are going to die. Her poverty is not because of her wickedness. There is no hint of that. Rather, it is because the social system has marginalized her and failed to provide a life-support system. Obviously then, as now, life-goods are given in adequate supply only to the competent, the productive, the well connected. She is none of these. So the gas has been turned off in her house. She shares what she has. But it is precious little.

Now we have seen that Elijah, in obedience to the Word, has made a striking gesture of solidarity. He has come to be with her. He submits himself to her circumstance. Her poverty is not glorified, but it is entered into as real. He quests in her circumstance to find a source for life. But his solidarity with her is more than a gesture of sympathy. It is a transformative gesture. His transformative act is in this speech: "Do not fear, use the little you have." The little, in the act of using it, is transformed and redescribed. In verse 14, the little is described according to the promise of God: "The jar of meal shall not be spent, and the cruse of oil shall not fail." And verse 15 ends tersely, "She went and did as Elijah said; and she . . . ate for many days."

Now there is something mysterious, odd, primitive, and inscrutable here. It may be only a wonder tale that only simple-minded people can tell. The story explains nothing. And neither shall I. The outcome is that the life-world of the widow is utterly changed. What had been a world of death becomes a season of life. Characteristically, such narratives cannot be explained. They can only be told and heard, decided on, and perhaps believed. It is not the person of Elijah that is prophetic for us. It is the narrative. It is the narrative that asserts that the world is not closed and the system is not absolute.

We recognize, of course, that this story has parallels to the feeding miracles of Jesus. That does not explain anything either. But the stories bear witness to the same subversive reality. The prophet is one who has the power, the authority, and the freedom to commit acts of life in a world that has been defined by death. When the prophet calls her to "fear not," he wrenches the woman out of the world of fear, fear that was a product of her marginality. What is she afraid of? Well, of death. But also of despising, of being emptied of power and dignity, of marauding soldiers and foreclosing lawyers and snooping social workers and loan sharks. She is set in a social world of terror. She is without friend, without advocate, utterly exposed and at the mercy of social agents whom she cannot understand.

In the middle of all this, there is holy power at work in Elijah. But let us not spiritualize. What Elijah does is to break the death grip of the dominant system. He acts against the social monopoly of those who control the means of production. The king is supposed to control bread and oil. Energy must be properly administered. With the king, it was all routine. He was the only source. But he had failed. That is what the whole narrative presumes, already with the drought in 17:1. The king could not cope with the energy crisis. The narrative destabilizes because it asserts that the official forms of power are not only dysfunctional, but in fact that they also bring death. Life will have to be sought and found elsewhere, outside the system that has failed. So a transformative gesture of solidarity turns out to be destabilizing. It declares that the dominant definition to reality is null and void. The king cannot give life. There are, however, sources of life that the king does not administer. Those have been retained by God alone. Every time this narrative is rightly told and faithfully heard it reenacts and replicates this nullification of the social system. One can tell that it continued to have such a power and attractiveness because Jesus uses it in Luke 4 and assumes that his listeners will catch the point. In Luke 4, Jesus is also seen as a destabilizing agent who renders the known world null and void. It is no wonder that they tried to stone him, because he enacted the destruction of their known world.

So a practical digression. Every community, every family, every congregation, every person has arranged a settlement of power and weakness. We know who has social power in a family.[9] We know in ordering our lives which sorts of things are honored and credited. We learn to compensate and adjust so that we "lead from strength." We live in those patterns so long that they appear absolute. The prophetic action is to speak a "fear not" at the point of weakness. When that "fear not" is sounded, one begins to notice new sources of life where none was noticed, new vitality that had been declared null and void. We can now notice on a clear day that some forms of social power we had trusted are in fact deeply dysfunctional. Now my point is that prophetic ministry is not limited to public policy and social action. It belongs to the liturgy and to pastoral care. It consists in finding life at the weak, discounted points of existence. When life is spotted there, the presumed power arrangements are threatened and destabilized because the monopoly is broken. The narrative invites us into a crisis in which old power arrangements are failed and new ones are being honored and found functional. And it is wrought by a "fear not" spoken at the moment of helplessness, a speech-promise that opens an alternative world.

Well, Elijah should have left then. He would have been ahead. But he did not get away in time. Soon the mother comes with her final loss. Now she has lost not meal or oil, but her only son, probably her only reason to scratch for life from day to day. She blames the prophet. Maybe you are good at giving meal and oil, she says. But you must also be the one who is a child-killer. It is odd reasoning. Perhaps the mother is hysterical. Or perhaps she senses what a destabilizing force he is and does not like it that close to home. Anyway, the agenda is now not hunger. It is death, as it always finally is with the marginal. The prophet is put in a situation of death to see if he can work life. Indeed, the entire narrative sets him against death and challenges his power. The question is, Who has the power of life? Those who have the forms of power do not have the power for life. King Ahab never raised anyone from the dead!

Elijah does not flinch. He takes the body of the boy. He seems to engage in some kind of physical gesture, perhaps artificial respiration. But what he finally does is pray. In the first scene, he addressed the woman, "Do not fear." Now he does not address the woman. Now he addresses God, the God who must be addressed in seasons of death. In verse 20, he cries out in anguish to God. He accuses God, even as the mother has accused him. In verse 21, he petitions God to let this child have life. He prays to God against the coldness of death because he does not believe that death is the last word. Notice how unencumbered and unarmed is this prophet. He has no resource, only prayer. Only the capacity to invoke the God of life in a season of death.

The narrative ends by having the prayer answered. God heard. The child lives. The woman trusts. This narrative, then, is an episode of *rehabilitation*,[10] which is the counter side of *destabilization*. The prophet engages not simply in an act of solidarity. He is not only willing to be there in this season of death. He transforms. He has power and authority to change circumstance because he trusts utterly the sovereign rule of Yahweh against the power of death. Now I do not want to over-interpret, but let me suggest this way of reading the text. Perhaps the story concerns the question, *Who has power for life?* The conventional answer that all of us give almost automatically and certainly uncritically is, "The system." That is what the system claims and that is what it exists for. But, of course, this widow has no access to that. The system is not for her. She receives no life from the royal apparatus of the legal establishment or the temple machinery. So her crisis is to see if there are forms of life available that fall outside administered forms. The narrative makes it unavoidable. The power for life is loose in the world. It is not contained by the king, who can cause no rain. But other kinds of folks, especially this prophet, have access to power for life.

That is how pastoring may be prophetic: To assert, to act on, live out the assurance that the power for life is worked by God in our midst and it will not be contained by our vested interests. The power for life is not controlled and contained in the normal, official channels. The monopoly is broken. The medical community does not control healing. The bureaucratic church does not govern grace. The agents of arms do not really preside over the possibilities of peace. The world is much more open than that to the invasion of God's life-giving power, granted to the unqualified.

One can recognize the echo of this story in Jesus' handling of the daughter of Jairus (Mark 5:22–24, 35–43). Of course, where Jesus is, the power for life is loosened. It will not be denied or monopolized. Every society has agents who imagine that they control and can dispense the power of life and that such a monopoly lends stability. This prophetic tale is destabilizing, because the power for life turns up in odd and unexpected places. Indeed, that is what the resurrection of

Jesus is about. It concerns the shattering of the monopolies around which life is organized and dispensed. So the early church can say that God raised up Jesus, because it was not possible that the bindings of death should hold him (Acts 2:24). We need to learn to read these life-surprising narratives with much more systemic awareness. They bear witness to the power for life at work in those undeserving places where we could not choose to administer life. Elijah seems to bear in his person the power for life that is always destabilizing in a world that has it all channeled in controlling ways. So the theological assertion is that God's power for life comes. The sociological statement is that the ones accustomed to administering life-goods do not control this. That evokes hostility, because the marginal, when enlivened, pose a social threat to those who benefit excessively from the present arrangement.

Audacious Clarification of Sovereignty

The second episode is better known to us, the contest at Mount Carmel (1 Kings 18–19). The theme I take is "The Audacious Clarification of Sovereignty." Now Elijah is not dealing with the poor. Now he is face to face with the regime, the king, the priests, the prophets, all the professionals, credentialed types. The crisis is a practical one that, on the face of it, does not seem to be theological. The problem is the drought. The drought hangs over the entire Elijah cycle, announcing that the royal enterprise is inept and dysfunctional. So the issue is, How do we get rain? Who has the capacity to make rain? Or, if you like, Is the government capable of handling the energy crisis, because lack of rain means failed energy? So there is an acute anxiety about rain, because that now becomes the issue of life and death. Likely, the polls revealed that 62 percent of the people regarded the threat of the drought to be the overriding public problem. It is somewhat analogous to the problem of security in our time. At least 62 percent of the people indicate that the nuclear threat is the

64

primary public issue. We have great debates about how to get security, who has the capacity to make us secure, and is the government capable of handling the matter.

You know how the narrative advances. It becomes a contest. Elijah is at his most audacious. He is so utterly convinced of the truth of his cause, of his God, that he dares to mock royal religion, to make fun of the sponsors, agents, and benefactors of the dominant system. He goes to extreme measures to set them up, all the more to humiliate them. For Elijah, and for the narrator, and for the listening community, the outcome is never in doubt; it is only dramatically suspended. The outcome is sure.

First, Elijah mocks their incapacity. He means to articulate that the system cannot deliver and cannot keep its promises. The king of the system, the priests and the prophets of the system, and finally the gods of the system cannot deliver (see the parallel startling conclusion on the Egyptian technicians in Exodus 8:18). The system cannot deliver, cannot keep its promises. Then he makes his own task as difficult as possible by pouring water on the fire before his prayers.

What the narrator has Elijah do is to see that the question of rain and energy is in fact a theological question of sovereignty. The question about the system is, *Can the gods of the system give life?* Is there an alternative source of life? Now the urging I make is that prophetic faith must be theologically intentional and explicit, knowing that the god-question is both open and urgent. That does not fit our stereotypes of the prophetic. But it is so. Conservatives tend to regard the god-question as settled and capable of reduction to a few formulae. Liberals tend to regard the god-question as trivial and unimportant. Elijah rejects both the liberal trivialization and the conservative reductionism because he believes that theology is important. To be sure, Elijah is not a systematic theologian spinning out theoretical tomes. But he is doing theology. He believes that in the thick of social conflict, the god-question is crucial because everything follows from it. My sense is that any of us who would be prophetic must take on ourselves the task of hard-nosed, intellectually disciplined theological work, because finally the real issues concern the question of sovereignty.

The poignant center of this episode is Elijah's question in 18:21: "How long will you go limping with two different opinions? If the Lord is God, follow him; but if Baal, then follow him." Prophetic faith holds for an either/or at the base of life. What is at issue here is not simply a theological label, as though the simple name of God matters. But we have rather a discussion about the relation between *the processes of life* and *the source of life*. Canaanite religion, Baalism, and indeed every civil religion, argues and presumes that the processes of life contain and are identical with the source of life. Being able to manage the process gives one control over the source. Now what this means practically is that the establishment— political, or religious, or scientific—has access to the processes and *can secure its own existence* by mastering the processes. Baalism is a religion that believes that the mystery of life has now been put at our disposal and that we have life on the terms we might like.

In the ancient world, when the temple was thought to be the seat of life, the priests were regarded as controllers of the sources of life. They were characteristically in the service of the king. Indeed, the history of the church reads in like manner with its tight control of sacraments as the access point of life, security, and well-being. In Jesus' time, the Torah was thought to be the source of life, and so arguments about the Torah become discussion on how to secure life on our own terms. In the modern world, the seduction of scientism and technology is that we have the capacity finally to administer life on our own terms. The arms race is a spin-off of that, for arms are an attempt to have our technology secure us. Every attempt, including some forms of process theology, runs the risk of this confusion of source and process.

Against all that, the hard-nosed Yahwism of Elijah makes a

radical distinction between source and process. The processes of rain, energy, and life may be discernible. But the source is hidden, inaccessible, and inscrutable. Rain will not be gotten by manipulation, but only by reference to the holy sovereign God, who is jealous. Therefore, all the techniques of religion, ritual, piety, morality, dogma, science, economics, whatever, are finally in vain. Because God will not yield to that. God has God's own person. God is not simply our own policy interests expressed in exaggerated form. God is an identifiable, known person, known in the liberating memory of the exodus. This God will give gifts, the gifts of life, but always on God's inscrutable terms that mock the pretentions and the mechanisms of the regime.

So the center of this prophetic act may be found in 1 Kings 18:36–37, where Elijah again resorts to prayer: "O Lord, God of Abraham, Isaac, and Israel, let it be known this day that thou art God in Israel, and that I am thy servant, and that I have done all these things at thy word. Answer me, O Lord, answer me, that this people may know that thou, O Lord, art God, and that thou hast turned their hearts back." As in the case of the dead child, the critical act is prayer, yielding, submitting, acknowledging. The result is a response (v. 38) that leads to praise and confession (v. 39). Finally, it is not technique, but petition. It is not management, but trustful asking that matters. Out of it emerges the awareness that God is not available and useful. The God of this prophet has no utilitarian value and cannot be harnessed into schemes for rain, for energy, for life, for security.[11] Now this prayer should not be trivialized. It is not an act of "spirituality." It is referring to life outside the system. It is driving the life-question back behind the processes to the source that is inaccessible. In such prayer, Elijah redescribes the world for himself and his contemporaries, and he enacts a claim for sovereignty that means to refute every false claim to sovereignty.

So prophetic faith has a stake in articulating the otherness, awfulness, holiness, sovereignty, jealousy of God, to keep final meanings at some remove from management practice and technical capacity. Indeed, it is God at some remove who permits critical reflection and the reception of an alternative. Note well, that the prophet is an alien in the world of his contemporaries, for he fails to live inside their rationality. Indeed, were he to concede their rationality, his capacity to pray and have power for life would surely be lost.

Prophetic faith resists the temptation to reduce God to a *technique*. God does not belong in any phrases that are concerned with "how to." In the ancient world, God is treated as though God were a technique for rain. In the modern world, God is treated as a technique for keeping families together, for keeping middle-class morality functioning, for the well-being of the Western alliance, for the maintenance of the free market system, for the soothing of a troubled psyche, and so on. Elijah's assault on Baalism is to assert that there is no essential or reliable linkage between the sovereign God and any technique for securing our existence or our well-being.

The push of prophetic faith is always to force a decision. The decision to be faced is not always immediately evident, because the decision most often seems to concern something other than theology. Prophetic faith is concerned to redefine the relation between heaven and earth, between God and creation, to insist that God is not an echo of creation or a client, but is in fact a free agent about whom a decision must be made.

It is worth thinking about technique and usability in our time. The pastor has access to many places in our common life where the truth of things is reduced to technique—about money, about relationships, about sexuality. In the world of technique, there is this audacious clarification of sovereignty. Life issues are about sovereignty. The question concerns what is finally real, to which everything else must be referred. And that, in this age of relativism, is so difficult because we prefer to think that there is no overriding reality, but only a series of little realities that we choose and like and fashion for ourselves. Sovereignty in any language—inclusive or exclusive—is so difficult for us, because we are dealing with a reality who has no analogy anywhere in our experience.

To articulate this holy one as really true is audacious, because it flies in the face of so much obvious pragmatism and utilitarianism. One must speak against the presumed data, for all the data is against this. But the data must be transformed to fit the claim. So Elijah's prayer returns to the roots. It goes back to the old tradition of Abraham, Isaac, and Jacob. The God addressed is the one who has always violated pragmatic reason. This God violated pragmatic reason in giving a birth to barren Sarah,[12] in freeing the slaves. Quite clearly, Elijah believes that this violation of technique and pragmatic reason is necessary to resolve the energy crisis.

It is clear to you, is it not, that such an audacious clarification of God's sovereignty is destabilizing? You see, this theology is serious stuff. We have treated theology as a leisure-time activity. But this theology serves to delegitimate the main claims of the royal system. The exposure of Baalism as gods who cannot give life is equivalent to nullifying the political, cultural authority of the regime. Prophetic theology concerns the unmasking of the idols that keep the system functioning. Prophetic ministry has these exposures to make. There are false claimants to power who must be delegitimated in order that the true God can have a say. So again I make the point. Prophetic ministry destabilizes to permit a newness that must be thoughtful and disciplined, a hard intellectual effort. The evidence that such an act is destabilizing is the resolve of Jezebel against Elijah: "So may the gods do to me, and more also, if I do not make your life as the life of one of them by this time tomorrow [19:2]." Who asserts the sovereignty of Yahweh asserts that *processes* do not give access to *source*. Who asserts sovereignty clashes with all the pseudosovereigns. But the reality of Yahweh's sovereignty has persuasion. It permitted people to make a life-receiving decision in 18:29. It did not, of course, persuade the regime, as indeed it hardly ever does.

Unseemly Interventions in Presumed Power Arrangements

The third dimension of Elijah's prophetic presence is in the well-known story of Naboth's vineyard (1 Kings 21). The rubric I use here is "Unseemly Interventions in Presumed Power Arrangements."

The narrative falls into two oddly related parts. In the first part, verses 1–16, the key actors are Naboth, Ahab, and Jezebel. Elijah is nowhere mentioned. It is possible to have narratives in Israel in which prophets are not present. But according to this tradition, when that happens, dimensions of humaneness disappear. The triangular interaction of the land-owner, the king, and the queen is not to be read as a personal struggle about greed. We shall understand the narrative more faithfully if we see that it is about the clash of land-tenure systems. Naboth embodies and is faithful to a system that is governed by patrimony, which assures him the inalienable rights, privileges, and responsibilities of his family inheritance. This vineyard could not be without Naboth belonging to it. Naboth could not be without this land. That close and inalienable land linkage is likely reflected in the jubilee practice (Leviticus 25), a social, institutional guarantee that this connection of land and family is indispensable for the functioning of society. It is less directly also a statement about the *materiality* of the human process. Human persons are intended to have land and turf as well as the social power that goes with them. When human persons lack land and social power, their persons are by that much diminished.

Conversely, Jezebel embodies a different land system, called prebendal.[13] We may in this context take that as a conventional Canaanite land system, perhaps specifically related to Tyre, from whence she came. This view sees land as a tradable commodity. But finally land is in the right of the king. There are no safeguards against the rapacious social policy of the strong against the weak. Obviously, the linkage of land and person is not inalienable, but a historical accident. All safeguards of egalitarianism are lost. Social power is distributed as one can seize it. This view offers a sharp contrast in economic theory to the view held by Naboth. Perhaps it finally offers a contrasting reading of human reality at the base in which some are entitled to social power over others, especially a monarch over the other landowners.

So the issue of the story is this: Who is entitled to what kind of social power in the form of land? Jezebel's ruthless and cunning action against Naboth shows that the release of rapacious possibility leaves none safe. Ahab is a pitiful figure in the middle. He is not an agent, but only a passive recipient. He knows better than does his queen about the rights of patrimony and how sacred they are in Israel. But he has neither the will to act on his own, nor the will to safeguard the practice of patrimony, nor the will to curb Jezebel.

So the story works out its course. It ends with Naboth dead for having resisted the unbridled will of the throne. And the last statement is closure, in verse 15: "Arise, take possession of the vineyard of Naboth the Jezreelite, which he refused to give you for money; for Naboth is not alive, but dead." Then the narrator concludes laconically, "As soon as Ahab heard that Naboth was dead, Ahab arose to go down to the vineyard of Naboth the Jezreelite, to take possession of it." End of story—it ends in death. Too many stories end that way, in death, usurpation, confiscation. The narrative ending in death tells not only about a clash of land systems, but also how it turns out. It is always death for the weaker at the hands of the stronger. The narrative describes a set of power relations that have stability and legitimacy. All parties assumed that the narrative was over and that it had ended on royal terms. It seems to be over for Naboth. Ahab and Jezebel also think it is over. The narrative seems ended. The land seems claimed. History seems closed. Everything seems so.

But Elijah is so unseemly. In fact, just as the narrative seems to end, this unseemly one starts the narrative underway again. Now in the second part of the narrative (vv. 17–29), things begin abruptly in a way that the royal partners did not suspect and could not resist: "Then the word of the Lord came to Elijah the Tishbite, saying, 'Arise, go down to meet Ahab.'" The word from Yahweh is quite explicit. It commissions Elijah to speak an entire lawsuit form, complete with indictment and sentence. Where there is a prophet, history can continue. Where there is a prophet, the narrative can continue, although now the narrative takes on a conflictual tone. Until verse 17, everything had been managed and covered over in seeming harmony. Now the same matters are unclosed, disclosed, and shown to be in deadly dispute.

Until this moment in the narrative, the presumed power arrangements had all been in favor of the royal couple. Nobody raised serious questions—until the Word, until the prophet. Elijah's speech, which is unseemly, if not treasonable, does not for a moment accept those power schemes. Elijah considers them illicit and in fact already nullified. The indictment puts it this way: "Thus says the Lord, 'Have you killed, and also taken possession? [v. 19].'" The question is rhetorical, the answer clear. This is followed by the sentence: "In the place where dogs licked up the blood of Naboth shall dogs lick your own blood [v. 19]." The lawsuit is dumped right into the middle of the narrative, even as the lawsuit is dumped inescapably into the middle of life. The abrasiveness of the lawsuit disturbs the presumed power arrangements. The premise of royal power is that there is no voice or agent bold enough to posit a lawsuit. Indeed, the speech of Elijah is only a rhetorical act. He seems to have no proper authority to make such a claim. But it turns out immediately to be a rhetorical act with immense destabilizing power. Its power is that on the face of it, it is true. No party in the narrative seems to doubt its validity. Jezebel is kept silent and invisible by the narrator. Ahab is moved to repentance. The truth of the lawsuit is so simple, yet so urgent. It asserts that Yahweh, not Jezebel, not Ahab, not Baal, nor the gods of Tyre, in fact, orders life. If Yahweh, then, in Israel this always refers one back to Torah. The lawsuit asserts that power must answer to covenantal rule. Specifically, there are in the Torah prohibitions of a nonnegotiable kind against murder and against usurpation (coveting). The power of the state is not absolute. The power of the powerful is not excessively regarded. The dominant system may have power to fashion its own world. But that fashioned world is always relative, always under scrutiny, always in jeopardy.

Power now, in the second part of the narrative, is deployed differently. It is not simply throne against Naboth. Now Yahweh intrudes as the key power agent in the narrative. There Yahweh enters; the power of the others seems irrelevant. The calculus is all shifted. Naboth has no ally who will save his life; it is too late for that. Naboth and his folk now have an avenger who will see that the blood of Naboth is honored in retaliation (cf. Genesis 9:6).

Regimes that absolutize their power tend to freeze the historical process and order life absolutely. There power of a social kind seems transcendent and beyond challenge. But power relations, so the prophet insists, are never as clean and simple as we imagine. The prophetic task is to reopen the power question, to ask, Who needs to have a say in this matter? This applies not only to the great public issues. I suggest that there is no pastoral encounter in which the redefinition of power relations is not an open problem. We are so caught up in our presuppositions that we fail to notice. But in so many ways, Elijah gives a paradigm which asserts that the cry of the "bruised reed" and the "dimly burning wick" (Isaiah 42:3) is never silenced, even as the cry of Abel from the ground is never silenced (Genesis 4:10), precisely because such folk have an advocate who will not quit. Elijah brings to speech the presence of that powerful, relentless advocate who will not let such deathliness go unanswered.

The narrative then moves to an exposition of the lawsuit, which is somewhat cryptic. But in verses 20–24, Elijah makes it plain, harshly plain. The lawsuit means the end of the dynasty, an ignoble end. The wonder may be that Ahab is still enough in touch with the tradition that he can repent (v. 27). But the repentance does not override the judgment. It only delays the matter one generation. The judgment is sure against such a false set of power relations.

Implications for Pastoral Ministry

Now Elijah is not the whole of the prophetic tradition. But for our context it offers some remarkable pointers for a pastoral ministry that is prophetic. I have focused on three narratives that suggest three characteristic prophetic agendas:

1. *Transformative gestures of solidarity,* in which Elijah brings life to a marginal widow, in a season of death

2. *Audacious clarification of sovereignty,* in which Elijah mocks the theological claims of the established power and permits a time of obedience to the true God

3. *Unseemly intervention in presumed power relations,* in which Elijah, by his powerful speech, shatters the closed power system and opens life to the relentless holiness of God.

Throughout this process of study I have asked myself, How was Elijah able to do this? Where did he get the courage, the freedom, the stamina, and the authority to enact such a ministry? We know that in 19:4–18 he was in a deep depression, because his great efforts seemed to make no difference, except to make him an exposed outcast. I do not minimize the problem, but I state it squarely so that we understand the "map" of prophetic ministry and are not surprised that it leads here. If I have rightly discerned the categories, this ministry of destabilization brings hostility as part of the territory. And I have suggested that all three of these acts are acts of destabilization.

I have a modest observation on the resources that are available to Elijah. At the outset of this narrative (17:3–6), in Yahweh's first address to him, he is given this initial command: "Depart from here and turn eastward, and hide yourself by the brook Cherith, that is east of the Jordan. You shall drink from the brook, and I have commanded the ravens to feed you there [vv. 3–4]." And the ravens did as commanded. At the outset, Elijah is commanded to the wilderness, to the same place where John the Baptist and, later, Paul went, to a place not unlike the setting for the temptations of Jesus.

So I suggest this: From the beginning, Elijah is commanded *to disengage from royal definitions of reality.* He is not to think the thoughts of the royal establishment. He is not to eat their food, hope their hopes, fear their fears. He is not to share their perceptions or participate in their rationality. He is to be one who lives in a different social rationality that is defined by the power and purpose of Yahweh. Elijah's freedom and authority stem from the fact that he did not perceive the world through royal categories. He owed no such allegiance and had no fear of conflict, because he had arrived at a different perception of truth. Surely, the key issue is *withdrawal from that rationality.* But the beginning point is *economic:* A different food supply (cf. Daniel 1; Mark 8:15). The key factor is not to be beholden economically, for then if one is not cared for and fed by them, one may more likely be free of the controlling perception of reality. I suggest that for all of us in our affluent society who yearn for the freedom and authority to be prophetic, we will find different modes of living only insofar as we disengage, intellectually and economically. After all, that disengagement from royal definitions of reality is what Jesus called for in summoning disciples and in proclaiming the Kingdom. And it is what we claim is at issue in baptism when we renounce loyalty to the rulers of this age.

Finally, I must make explicit what I have implied about pastoral care. I know well that "frontal" prophetic ministry of a stereotypical kind is not our agenda. Maybe it should be, but it is not. I hope that what I have said relates to pastoral care broadly conceived in all its dimensions. So let me say it two ways.

First, I intend to argue that the agenda of Elijah is the agenda of all serious pastoral ministry, which includes, but is not limited to, pastoral counseling. Much pastoral ministry has been preoccupied, in my judgment too singularly, with psychological matters. But there is now a move away from that in the field. The urging I make is that these three issues of solidarity with the *marginal*, clarity about *sovereignty*, and *renewed power relations* belong to a biblical understanding of health. Any pastoral care that shrinks from these matters is likely to be romantic, trivial, and irrelevant to the real health issues facing us.

One can ask about marginality in one's own person (cf. the use made of such an analogy in 1 Corinthians 12:14–25). One can pursue power relations in marriage or in any other social unit. One can reflect on sovereignty in any part of one's personal or interpersonal life. These are not alien categories. But they are categories of concern that have been neglected by modernity. But they will not go away, because they are the real issues. What matters is that the claim of covenant with the Holy God gives us a different agenda from self-help and adjustment theories of well-being. My sense is that in U.S. society we have adopted models of psychological health that will finally destroy us. There is in this a discernment of human reality that gives us peculiar access for the real issues and, I dare say, peculiar resources for responses that are genuinely healing and restorative.

Second, the modes in which this textual material may be helpful are many and varied. I do not suggest that one ought (or can) stand up and announce prophetic lawsuits. Indeed, I have insisted from the beginning that our work is not to replicate Elijah, but to let these texts have their full say. My hunch is this: If we get clear on what the real issues are—marginality, sovereignty, power relations—we will begin to see many ways in which these issues can be pursued. Pastoral care requires enormous intentionality, so that in every circumstance of preaching, liturgy, public prayer, wherever, the real human issues are raised.

The dichotomy of prophetic and pastoral is a misunderstanding of both. I can think of no one in our tradition who is more intensely engaged in pastoral care than Elijah. He practices it with the widow by being present in her need. He practices it with the false prophets by exposing their fraud and permitting a faithful confession. He practices it with the king by telling the truth. And in each case, as Yahweh's sovereignty is celebrated, the power for life is present—even to Ahab. The unleashing of the power for life in this world bent on death depends on pastoral work that is rigorous and prophetic work that is passionate. But such pastoral-prophetic work requires being fed by ravens, not at the king's table.

CHAPTER 4

The Prophetic Task of Pastoral Ministry: The Gospels

John Howard Yoder

PROPHETISM CAN BE DEFINED AS THAT UNDERSTANDING OF history that finds meaning in the concern and purpose of God, for that history and the participation of God in that history. One might do well, in some context, to invest some time in unpacking the assumptions and implications of this way of putting the question. What would be the alternative understandings? Would there be a God who would not care about history and not act in it? Or a God who would act within it without caring about it? Or who would care without acting? Does it make a difference which history one is talking about? Is there only one history, namely, something like "history as a whole" or "history as such"? Or is history necessarily particular, so that the God who called the Jews might not be identical with the God of whom the Bantus speak? Is the choice of histories itself a choice of Gods?

For present purposes, however, one must lean in the other

John Howard Yoder, Ph.D., is professor of theology at the University of Notre Dame, Notre Dame, Indiana.

direction. I seek here simply to disengage from the Gospel narrative a description of the specific ways in which Jesus said his "Father" cared for and intervened in the life of people.[1]

If we were conversing with Platonism or with Buddhism, it might be appropriate to discuss *whether* God is interested in history. From some religious and philosophical perspectives, the question may be whether God can care about history: whether it is compatible with the nature of Deity to be concerned about the realm of the finite and the particular. Is not Deity, by definition, infinite and incompatible with taking with ultimate seriousness any one time, any one place, any one practical goal, any one set of people?

That is not a question which can be meaningfully addressed to the Gospel accounts; they stand on the shoulders of centuries of Hebrew history, where that question had been resolved with such resounding certainty as not to be a possible question. The question that was evident from the perspective of Greek or Roman antiquity and that in the West became visible again in the age of Enlightenment—"how odd of God to choose the Jews"—did not strike the Gospel writers as odd at all. That Yahweh of Hosts cares about a particular people is the specific definition, the identity of Yahweh, as the One who chooses to be and to bring into being, more than it is a description of anything meritorious or lucky about the lineage of Abraham. Jesus presupposes and prolongs that understanding of the uniqueness of Yahweh as the one who chooses.

The story, however, dealing with the Jew Jesus between the Zealots and the Romans, between the Essenes and the Sadducees, does not show him as being tested or tempted to conceive of God as not in history. The questions were in *which* history and in which *direction*, toward what end, that caring divine intervention was to be discerned and obeyed.

In this essay, I discuss the witness of the Gospel texts themselves: It cannot be my task to seek to reach past the specific texts into the critical reconstruction and deconstruction of the events or the redactional processes behind them. A gospel is,

79

by nature, a witnessing document, and it is that dimension of witness that we want to hear. Rather than distill from the Gospel accounts a few timeless generalizations about a vision for history, I propose to review a series of the more dramatic vignettes within the narrative. Each implies and affirms certain deep certainties about God's intention for the human story.

The Promise Is Fulfilled

The private beginning of Jesus' ministry, according to three of the Gospel accounts, was a conversation with Satan in the desert, after Jesus had been baptized (like many other people) by John. What was being tested was his understanding of the way in which he was to proceed to be the liberator-designate. Will he do it as showman, as thaumaturgic welfare distributor, as multiplier of loaves and fishes? Will he do it by appearing suddenly in the temple to claim effective sovereignty, in the style of the Maccabees? Will he enter into a pact with the powers already ruling the globe?

None of these options would take Jesus or his people out of history. None of them would denature history as unimportant over against some other realm or kind of being. Jesus' answer is in the same world. It is a concrete alternative to those forms of the messianic temptation. His way will be an alternative to the way of the demagogue sweeping crowds along by his unique power, to that of the Zealot seizing the city by surprise violence, and to that of the collaborator scheming his way into the existing structures' domination.

The way of the demagogue, the Zealot, or the Herodian collaborator is not set aside because his goal of serving God's purposes is too concrete, or too historical, or too "political," but because it is historical differently. It is that differentness for which Jesus was first to live quietly half a lifetime in simple subordination to the Galilean family structure, from which he then emerged as a self-educated rabbi (something of a contra-

80

diction in terms) and peripatetic prophet, and, finally, by living just as he did, gathering disciples just as he did, dying just as he did, and rising just as he did to plant in the midst of history a new kind of social phenomenon. He reformulated what it means to be the people of God in the world.

The Platform

According to Luke's Gospel, the first milestone of Jesus' public ministry was the time when, in his hometown synagogue, he was given the scroll of Isaiah to read. It was already open, or he turned it open, to chapter 61 (vv. 1–2), where Messiah is speaking:

> The Spirit of the Lord is upon me,
>   because the Lord has anointed me
>   to bring good tidings to the afflicted;
> he has sent me to bind up the brokenhearted,
> to proclaim liberty to the captives,
> and the opening of the prison to
>   those who are bound;
> to proclaim the year of the Lord's favor.

There is no way to take history in general or God in general more seriously than to say of a divine promise, as Jesus did in Nazareth: "Today this word is fulfilled among you."

History is a process in which specific events can be identified as links in the chain leading from God's past to our common future. What it was that was fulfilled, according to this prophetic text, was the promise of a transformed set of human relations involving the forgiveness of debts, the liberation of prisoners, and the renewal of the agrarian economy. What the Authorized Version translated impenetrably by "the acceptable year of the Lord" clearly meant in the Isaiah text the promulgation of the year of Jubilee, the arrangement under which, in the Mosaic order, every family would be reinstated every half-century in the possession of their ancestral land. If their fathers had lost it through bad luck, it would be restored to them; if they had come into wealth because of their fathers' astuteness, they would give it back as a celebration of the year of grace.

Such a vision is obviously not a literal model for other times and places. It presupposed the patterns of kingship and of landholding of ancient Israel, giving no guidance (if taken with picayune literalism) for urban economies or for the landless. Jesus' vision was not antiquarian. It would be equally inappropriate to read with picayune literalism the analogous vision of the book of Micah, according to which all people will be unafraid, owning their own vines and fig trees, and to complain that it would not be an interesting promise for the Wheat Belt. What counts is the simplicity with which both visions use the stuff of common economic reality to concretize the divine presence.

This direct description of liberation as the assignment of Messiah, and as the mark of this present instant, lays claim on the historical moment in a more radical way than do those eschatological visions that project unthinkable cosmic catastrophes in the distant or even the imminent future. Jesus is saying that a new quality of human life is beginning to be operative in his time and place: in Nazareth and, more broadly, in Galilee, and all the way to Jerusalem in those weeks and months when his presence will force decision on his listeners. The decision his presence imposes is for or against a new order that can be likened to the new beginning prescribed by the "year of the Lord's favor." That proclamation was unacceptable in Nazareth: It rejected the insider privilege of those who thought of themselves as especially God's people.

The Precursor's Doubts

The prefaces to all three of the Synoptic Gospels report Jesus' baptism at the hands of John as the beginning of his public ministry. Luke's Gospel reports a more formal crossing of the threshold from the age of John to that of Jesus, when emissaries from John visit Jesus while John is in prison to allay John's doubts about whether what Jesus was achieving was what John had been predicting.

Jesus had been one with John in the confidence that the impact of the promised kingdom was to be a profound reversal: the ax at the root of the tree, the unproductive branches thrown to the fire, the flail attacking the threshing floor, the chaff being blown off to burn. . . . That is what makes of John's question a most fitting challenge: "Are you the one to come, or do we wait for another?" The question makes clear that the framework of historical meaning is a temporal expectation, which a given historical figure can either live up to or fail to live up to. The present moment is or is not the time of fulfillment.

Jesus accepted the question but did not answer it with a sentence or a "yes." He answered by pointing to events in process, to miracles of healing. That kind of healing, it appears, should sustain the faith of those who were probably looking for a different kind of liberation.

Detailed biographical or historical reconstruction, to the extent to which scholars can risk it at all, points up differences between contrasting pictures of what various people thought John might have wanted and what Jesus wanted: Was John more like a Zealot or an Essene? Were the connections between the two movements or the two men as direct as Luke says? How do we interpret the difference between the Lucan account, with the appearance of a positive transition from John to Jesus, and the picture that John's Gospel gives of some competitiveness between the two movements, and some need for the disciples of Jesus to disavow John in order to affirm Jesus? We need to name those questions as part of the necessary seriousness of real history; yet for the purposes of this essay, they do not matter. In any case, the Gospel account affirms a sequence of historic projects in which precursor and successor both understand God to be working in

83

the real world to establish justice. Neither gives an independent value to contemplative or ritual religion, even though both men spent long seasons in solitude and both laid claim to immediate understanding of the identity and purpose of God characterized by an immediacy quite different from the religions of tradition and authority. Their witness is not like what the "social gospel" vision of sixty years ago proposed by way of the reduction of religion to ethics. What they bring is not a reduction, but a rise to a higher power. They offer not "ethics" in the sense of a set of behavioral imperatives for good people, but the proclamation of a new social possibility for the human story. Both of them affirmed the real alternatives of first-century Palestine as the place where, thanks to a renewed transcendent intervention, God's will is known and achieved.

Jesus both does and does not take over the mantle and the prophetic style of his cousin John. His answer to the emissaries from John who asked whether he is what John was looking for, is affirmative; yet the evidence that he tells John's disciples should convince their leader is his own ministry of healing, not his projected take-over of the palace. He does not even join John in scolding Herod for his blatant public and probably politically motivated immorality. He does not let his prophetic mission be downgraded into telling rulers what not to do. Yet he is with John in seeing what he is doing as an alternative to the way the elders proceed.

The King in the Desert

The hinge of the public ministry of Jesus, to the extent to which creative historical empathy can reconstitute anything of the way in which that ministry might have developed, is the feeding of the multitude. Until then, the crowds following Jesus were mixed in their composition and their expectations. His closest disciples are described as not yet understanding the core of what he was proclaiming. The miracle of the loaves and fishes had fulfilled in powerful public drama the prediction of the tempter: If Jesus would feed the people, if in the face of the privation and vulnerability that being in the desert has always meant for the human organism Jesus were to provide abundant sustenance for the body, he would be accredited as the coming king. John's Gospel, the most interpretative account, makes that most clear. This event is the peak of the readiness of the crowds to acclaim Jesus as their anointed liberator. This had to mean (although our habits of interpretation have hitherto not taken it very seriously) that they would also be committed to supporting him in the military defense, against the Romans, of the kingdom they wanted him to set up. Now, for the first time, Jesus directly rejects that prospect. Now, for the first time, he tells his disciples of his coming suffering in ways that they are unable to understand and unwilling to accept. It is not that Jesus withdraws from having a messianic project for his people. It is that that project is defined with increasing clarity in ways that reject the temptations of holy violence. He joins the rabbis who had already decided that the Maccabean experiment had been a mistake. He prefigures a later rabbi like Jochanan Ben Zakkai, who was to disavow the Zealot rebellion of 66–70. That did not mean acquiescence in the Sadducean strategy of negotiation with the Romans within the framework of colonial status. It did not mean Essene quietism. For the present, Jesus does not say what alternative social project his message will mean. It has, in any case, meant a renewed claim to the mantle of Moses as the instrument of God's sustaining the people with bread in the desert, at the beginning of a new exodus.

The Disciple's Choice

For Luke's account, the most dramatic statement of the alternative way toward which Jesus has been leading his disciples since the episode of the loaves in the desert is chapter 14. The sequence of accounts that describe Jesus' movement toward Jerusalem (chap. 9) had been marked along the way with reminders of his political vision. At the beginning of chapter 13 are two references to episodes of Zealot violence: the incident of the tower of Siloam and the massacre of some Galileans by Pilate. "Great multitudes" are still following Jesus (14:25); it is to them that he addresses his dramatic warning against a too-easy decision to join his movement. Anyone who will follow him must be ready to jeopardize immediate nuclear family loyalties. The phrase he uses is "hate his own father and mother." Certainly this reference to division within the family does not mean preoccupation with psychic problems of internal family dynamics. It is, rather, that the unity of the family as the basic social cell is sacrificed to the values of the larger social cause to which a follower of Jesus becomes committed. That cost is also described as the loss of one's own life. The way one might lose one's own life is described as one's "own cross." The "cross" in that connection can obviously not mean what it has come to mean in later Protestant pastoral care; neither the inward suffering of struggle with self nor the outward suffering of personal ill health or difficult social relations. The "cross" could only mean (in the setting that Luke's account means to narrate) what the Romans were wont to do with people threatening their political hegemony. Jesus is warning the crowd that to follow him means exposing oneself to the reproach of causing political unrest. He goes on to reinforce the warning against too lighthearted an adhesion to his cause with two anecdotes of public figures who found, to their shame, that they could not complete an ambitious project they had undertaken: a building project and a war. King Herod had just done both these things. If he had been speaking in March 1984, Jesus might have referred to an astronaut who thought he could get himself nominated to the Presidency, or to a President who thought he could pacify Beirut militarily. Better not to set out for battle if you are not ready to give your life for the cause. What more dramatic statement could there be of the irrevocably historical shape of Jesus' project?

The Liberator's Choice

The most outright and overt explanatory statement that Jesus gives at any point is probably his word to the disciples in the upper room. Luke has placed here in the middle of the passion account a word that in Matthew and in Mark is found at other points in Jesus' ministry. It is framed between the breaking of bread, in which Judas' betrayal is foretold, and two other words about rejection: the prediction of Peter's denial and the word about the two swords. Certainly we are not pressing the text when we understand Luke to be illuminating all those conflict words with this one general teaching, and illuminating the teaching with the words of conflict. When Jesus says, "The kings of the Gentiles exercise lordship over them; and those in authority over them are called benefactors [22:25]," he is describing his own temptation. When he says, "But not so with you; rather let the greatest among you become as the youngest, and the leader as one who serves [22:26]," he is describing not only his own decision about his own path, but also the prophetic perspective on the moral resolution of conflict. He is restating, in the form of a moral teaching, his own choice, which he had been making and renewing weekly since his baptism, and day by day from the triumphal entry until that upper room conversation, and which he would be renewing again that night in the garden. It is the choice between violence claiming to be sanctified by the good it promises to do (those in authority calling themselves benefactors) and the authentic good done by one who serves.

Jesus thereby first of all makes clear that his fundamental choice in this world was how to be that kind of benefactor. At the dramatic turning point of this passion Passover, he best

87

describes his path by contrasting it—but that also means comparing it—with what the rulers of the peoples claim to do. He does not suggest that he has an alternative way to be a priest, although later Christians rounded out their picture of him by saying that too. He does not claim to be a better prophet, although he acknowledges the line of prophets culminating in John as his precursors. Later Christians have properly also used the language of "prophet," as this book does, to describe his achievement. Yet the comparison and contrast with which he does define his mission is that of kingship. They claim to be benefactors; he claims to be benefactor. They claim to be great; he provides an alternative vision of greatness. They dominate; he serves; and there is no more profound description of what he asks of his disciples than that they be servants, with him and in his way.

That contrast is not meant as one moral hint among many. It is not merely one scrap of political wisdom among others. It is a capsule statement of Jesus' own key self-definition, as he was torn between quietistic and Zealot models of the messianic role. The difference is not simply between ways to run a battle or ways to be socially responsible. It is between definitions of salvation.

What we learn from Jesus is not a suggestion about strategy or skill in the discharge of those particular leadership responsibilities ordinarily associated with the pastorate. What the gospel tells us is rather what kind of world we are called to minister in and toward.

In a world of greed and self-aggrandizement, whose technology and dominant philosophy foster selfishness more than ever before, the people of God, as a whole, are called to be the first fruits of an age of redistribution and shared sufficiency.

In an age of rampant and in fact renascent nationalisms and of imperialisms whitewashed with the ideology of liberty, we are called to be heralds and instruments of the one world already created at the cross and at Pentecost, whose ultimate triumph we are to proclaim despite its evident present defeats.

Yet what is most striking about the way in which Jesus serves those goals is not the stated ends—which many another sage had dreamed about and many another activist promoted. What is original and redemptive is that he does it with his own blood; that the community he creates is the product and not the enforcer of that new regime. His followers will live from, not toward, the victory of Christ. Our life is to proclaim, not to produce, the new world.

The series of vignettes could be extended through the rest of the Gospel accounts and on through Acts; but for now, with this word from the upper room, we leave the narrative and move to analysis.

Not Engineering, but Doxology

The standard account of the challenge of social concern would have us believe that the most difficult problem is to describe with some precision what kind of world we want: Do we want property to be owned socially or privately? Do we want prices to be set by the marketplace or in some other way? Do we want decisions to be made by an aristocracy or by a referendum? Do we want the races to mix or to live at peace apart? Once those broad goals have been set, the standard account of our social ethical agenda would have us believe that the rest is only a matter of engineering, of bringing to bear toward that end whatever power we have available. Those who know which way the course of events should go can, with moral propriety, push them in that direction, and the clearer they are about that direction, the more authority they have to take control. The worse the situation is, the more violently they have right to take over.

Jesus does not reshape the question by choosing a different social goal behind which to place his prophetic authority. His social goal is utterly traditional: It is that of the Mosaic corpus, with its bias toward the sojourner, the widow, and the orphan. It is that of Isaiah and Micah, the vision of a world taught the arts of peacemaking because they have come to Jerusalem to learn Torah and to hear the judicial oracles of Yahweh. It is the ingathering of the nations in the age of the anointing. What differs about Jesus is not a different goal: It is that he sees, for both himself and his disciples, a different mode of implementation. They are not to be content with the existing order, as if it were close enough to what Yahweh wants that one could get from where we are organically to where Yahweh wants to take us. It is not the path of the quietists or the Essenes, who went to the desert to wait for God to act, or of the Pharisees, who kept themselves pure within society, disavowing the present world's structures, but leaving it to a future divine intervention to set them straight. It is not the path of Zealot presumption, claiming to be the party of righteousness authorized by God to trigger the coming of the new age through a paroxysm of righteous insurrection. Each of those standard type responses to "the mess the world is in" is a different answer to the question, "How do *we* get from here to there?" Jesus' alternative is not to answer that question in a new way, but to renew, as the prophets had always been trying to do, the insistence that the question is how to get from there to here. How can the lordship of Yahweh, affirmed in principle from all eternity, be worthily confessed as grace through faith? How can the present world be rendered transparent to the reality already there, that the sick are to be healed and the prisoners freed? We are not called to love our enemies in order to make them our friends. We are called to act out love for them because at the cross it has been effectively proclaimed that from all eternity they were our brothers and sisters. We are not called to make the bread of the world available to the hungry; we are called to restore the true awareness that it always was theirs. We are not called to topple the tyrants, so that it might become true that the proud fall and the haughty are destroyed. It already is true;

we are called only to let that truth govern our own choice of whether to be, in our turn, tyrants claiming to be benefactors.

It is thus a profound misapprehension of the messianic moral choice to think that in his rejection of violence, Jesus was led by methodological purism in moral choice, choosing to be an absolutist about the sacredness of life. It would be an equally profound misapprehension to think that he was the world's first Gandhian, calculating the prospects for a social victory as being in his particular circumstances greater for nonviolent than for violent tactics. Both of those interpretations of what Jesus was doing as a social strategist follow the "standard account of social ethical discernment" that it is precisely the purpose of all the prophets to free us from. Jesus' acceptance of the cross, from which we throw light on his rejection of both pietism and Zealot compulsion, was not, in the first analysis, a moral decision, but an eschatological one. It was dictated by a different vision of where God is taking the world. Or, we may say that it was an ontological decision, dictated by a truer picture of what the world really is.

As a final exercise in clarification, perhaps the originality of the prophetic vision of Jesus can be brought out by an effort to contrast it with the other models that have tended to dominate this discussion and to teach us how to think.

For four centuries now, it has been especially the Lutheran believers who have tirelessly reminded us that in soteriology we are not supposed to achieve, but to trust. Salvation is not a product, but a presupposition. We do not bring it about, but we accept it as a gift of grace mediated through faith. Jesus and the early disciples did not let that understanding dictate for them only what to do about "salvation," in the sense of the present integrity or the ultimate destiny of the soul. They applied it as well to shalom as the social historical purpose of Yahweh. We do not achieve it so much as we accept it. It is not as basic to engineer it as to proclaim it.

For still longer than the Lutherans, Roman Catholics, or at least the schoolmen among them, have been concerned to clarify that nature and grace stand not in opposition, but are integrated in a complementary or organic way. The behavior God calls for is not alien to us; it expresses what we really are made to be. Yet, unfortunately, later Catholic strategy has foreshortened the critical potential of that vision by confusing the "nature of things" with the way they are now in the fallen world, especially in ethnic and national definitions of community and patriarchal definitions of order. When society has been defined as the nation and social order as patriarchy, then it is no longer true that grace completes nature; in the face of that definition of "nature," the word of Yahweh has to be like a fire, like a hammer that breaks rocks into pieces. Yet when the "nature of things" is properly defined, the organic relationship to grace is restored. The cross is not a scandal to those who know the world as God sees it, but only to the gentiles, who look for what they call wisdom, or the Judeans, who look for what they call power. This is what I meant before, when I stated that the choice of Jesus was ontological: It risks an option in favor of the restored vision of how things really are. It has always been true that suffering creates shalom. Motherhood has always meant that. Servanthood has always meant that. Healing has always meant that. Tilling the soil has always meant that. Priesthood has always meant that. Prophecy has always meant that. What Jesus did—and we might say it with reminiscence of scholastic Christological categories—was that he renewed the definition of kingship to fit with the priesthood and prophecy. He saw that the suffering servant is king as much as he is priest and prophet. The cross is neither foolish nor weak, but natural.

A form of Catholic moral discernment older than the scholastic vision is the culture of the early medieval period, between the old Caesars and the new Carolingians, an age during which civilization had to survive without the preferred vehicle of righteous royalty. If you look at that epoch with the eyes of Justinian or of Charlemagne, it was the "dark ages." If, however, we ask of those ages what kind of light people had to

92

live by, the answer is that it was the culture of the saints. Moral education was a matter of telling the stories of holy people. Holiness included patterns of renunciation and withdrawal, but it was also the age when a hermit would be called from his cave or an abbot from his monastery to be made a bishop. It was an age when the bishop, through his control of the sacrament of absolution, was the community's main moral teacher and, through his administration of the right of sanctuary, was its most solid civil peacekeeper.

It has been one major impoverishment of our Western moral universe that first the schoolmen and then the reformers, the former looking for something more intellectually generalizable and the latter denouncing abuses, have robbed us of the place of hagiography in morality. Not only did that mean a loss of the human concreteness of biography as a way to talk about being human. It also led to forgetting wholeness. It predisposed us to pulling love apart from justice, purity from practicality, and leadership from servanthood, dichotomies that have dominated moral analysis ever since. When God chose Jesus as the way to come into the world, when Jesus chose disciples as a way to make his message mobile, and when the disciples chose the "gospel" as preferred literary form of witness, each meant the choice of the story of the holy one as the dominant prototype not only of communicating, but of being good news. Jesus' parables, like his presenting himself as model, did not represent a mere pedagogical choice of "storytelling" as a more understandable way to communicate to illiterate crowds; the story is rather in the order of being and in the order of knowing the more fundamental mode of reality.

Yet older than our teachers from the "dark ages" is the Hebrew heritage which taught generations of Jews and Christians that law is the form of grace. Christians have been busy since the second century with weakening that awareness. Hellenistic apologetes felt that the Jewishness of Torah would keep them from reaching nonbelievers. Reformers feared it

93

would let religious performance stand in the way of saving grace. Both of these forms of anti-Judaism have profoundly impoverished us. It is only now, in the shadow—or should we say in the light—of the Hitlerian holocaust, that we are beginning to renew the recognition of all that was lost with the Jewishness of the original meaning of Jesus. Jesus' insistence, at the center of the Sermon on the Mount, which is itself the literary-catechetical center of the Gospel account as structured by Matthew, that the law is fulfilled and not forgotten is indispensable to understanding his claims in his time and even more for our time. Thinking that we are freed *from* the law instead of *through* and *for* the grace of Torah is at the root of the anomie of our age, even though regrettably most of the preachers who proclaim that sorry truth seem to be interested in restoring a law that was not fulfilled in the Sermon on the Mount, one that would not relativize the family and favor the outsider.

The point of these side glances at the Lutheran, the scholastic, the hagiographical, and the nomic visions has been not to reject them as wrong, but to englobe and transcend them as true but inadequate. To make the claim with the simplicity of caricature: The prophetic vision does more wholly what each of those other modes seeks to do. Its vision of the priority of grace is more fundamental than that of the Lutheran mode, since it applies justification by grace through faith to morality as well as to "salvation"—or, as I hinted earlier, because its picture of the shalom that is given us by grace is both morality and what used to be called "salvation." It affirms the nature of things "more profoundly than the scholastic vision because it reads the substantial definition of nature from the incarnation and holy history, not from medieval culture or Greek philosophy. It affirms and transcends the culture of saintliness by planting in our midst the magnetic story of the model of all models, whom to follow is first of all a decision and a path before it becomes goals and principles. It fulfills the vision of the law of God by focusing the deep meaning of

94

not swearing falsely, not committing adultery, loving the neighbor not as a mere holding pattern to save the civil order, but as the design for restoring the cosmos.

Cop-out or Pars pro Toto?

If the gospel logic does not follow the standard account in centering the ends of Christian historical concern in the specific project to be achieved through the prophets' influencing the bearers of power, and if the model of the cross remains normative both in its particular historical orientation to the man Jesus and in its principled renunciation of coerciveness in implementation, is this not some kind of otherworldly quietism?

The possibility has always been open that it could be read that way. It is intrinsically not that; they do not crucify quietists. A more adequate description would be to say that in its most formative stages this view is "apocalyptic"; but to sort out the multiple meanings that that term has in recent usage would be beyond our scope. What can be said most simply is that the future toward which the prophet knows God has already effectively begun to move the world is prefigured in the possibilities offered and to some modest extent fulfilled in the believing community. Sometimes it is the Holy Spirit, sometimes it is the church that the apostolic writings refer to as the *arrabon* (the pledge, or down payment) or as the "first fruits" of God's impending victory. Here already the lame are healed, here the underdog is honored, here bread is shared and ethnicity is transcended.

The people of God are not a substitute or an escape from the whole world's being brought to the effective knowledge of divine righteousness; the believing community is the beginning, the pilot run, the bridgehead of the new world on the way. Its discourse may be called "apocalyptic" if by that— without disregard for other meanings the term may have—we designate a portrayal of the way the world is being

95

efficaciously called to go that does not let present empirical readings of possibility have the last word.

I have used the phrases "believing community" and "people of God" instead of the other apostolic term *ecclesia,* because one learns from the literature concerned with this theme that reference to the community is often taken pejoratively; that is, the term church is often defined not by the apostolic and prophetic vision, but by the abuses of sectarian, triumphalist, or ritualistic experience of the past.

None of those abuses is founded in what the prophets, Jesus, and the apostles were talking about. The believing community is the epistemological prerequisite of the prophetic confession. Whether it is God's intent to restore the world does not depend on faith, but faith is an instrumental precondition of knowing the shape of that restoration and defending it from our own foreshortened perspectives, whether foreshortened by selfishness or shame or by a too simple hope or a too weak one. As Yahweh could use famine and pestilence, Midianite merchants, and pagan emperors for his purposes in the Hebrew story, so tomorrow we may be confident that powers beyond the confines of faith can be instruments of judgment and of construction; yet to confess and celebrate that work, the prophetic function of the confessing community is indispensable.

By the nature of the case, the life of this kind of community cannot be cared for only by one specialized functionary named "the pastor"; that understanding of the pastoral task would be a contradiction in terms. How such a community would be appropriately structured, in the diversity of ministries or charismata distributed by the Holy Spirit, can, however, not be unfolded on the basis of the Gospel texts. For the Gospel texts, Jesus himself is the shepherd.

Nonetheless we do well to recognize that as the messianic community continues to minister to a still not-yet-messianic age, there will be need, in order to maintain and propagate the community and to illuminate its interfaces with "the world," for skills and perspectives that our parlance calls "pastoral," focusing on a style more than an office. The bearer of the prophetic task is the whole people of God. Specific ministerial gifts within that work are to be measured by their congruence with the whole community's calling to be the advance agents of the coming realm. Each of the partial perspectives we have recognized—vocation, nature, sanctification, law—will call for specific people to help articulate the shape of the prophecy needed. Scribes will need to be "pastoral" rather than legalistic. Elders will need to be "pastoral" rather than patriarchal. Prophets will need to be "pastoral" rather than neurotic. Teachers will need to be "pastoral" rather than abstruse. The one who consoles will need to be "pastoral" rather than manipulatively therapeutic. Those who plan and lead assemblies for worship and those who "preach" will need to point beyond themselves to the realm, and beyond the esthetic to the prophetic. In our age's thought forms, the term most apt to preserve this accent will probably not be "pastor," with its overtones of professionalism and privilege; the place of the cross as a model for ministry will often better be rendered by the language of servanthood. Yet watching our language is not enough; "service" or "ministry" can also come to mean privilege.

The closest the Jesus of the Gospel accounts came to projecting the shape of the church was the description in Matthew (18:15–20) and in John (14—16, 20:19–23) of the coming guidance of the Paraclete to empower forgiveness and discernment. That is the warrant for continuing prophetic clarity. It is also the reason that the shape of the ministries contributing to that clarity must be renewed in every age. This is not a blank check for future impulsive, intuitionistic, or situationist "flexibility," for the Spirit's task is to remind the disciples of Jesus. The "more truth" that the Spirit interprets is coherent with its origin. Yet its coherence is not timeless rigidity; it is like that of a plant's organic growth, the implementation of a new regime. For this all the ministries in the body will be drawn on. Yet here I have let Jesus' pointers send us beyond the Gospels to the Epistles, beyond annunciation to unfolding.

The doctrine of the two natures of the Divine Son, enshrined in the formulae of Chalcedon, has come to be a metaphysical puzzle. Yet what these notions originally meant, and should still mean, is that God takes history so seriously that there is no more adequate definition of God's eternal purposes than in the utterly human historicity of the Jew Jesus. That same prophetic condescension makes of the believing community, of the human historicity of those who confess Jesus' normativeness, God's beachhead in the world as it is, the down payment, the prototype, the herald, the midwife of the New World on the way. The ultimate test of whether we truly believe that God's purposes are for the whole world, that they are knowable, that they are surely about to be fulfilled is whether we can accept that in the present age it is the circle of his disciples who by grace are empowered to discern, more visibly and more validly than the Caesars and the Cromwells, what it means when at his command they pray, "Your kingdom come, your will be done on earth as in heaven."

CHAPTER 5

Paul, Prophet and Spiritual Leader

George W. MacRae

THIS ESSAY REFLECTS ON THE PROPHETIC ROLE OF MINIS-
try as exemplified in the writings of Paul. The model is Paul
himself, who only indirectly claims such a prophetic role.
After a brief discussion of Paul as apostle—for him, the most
sensitive issue of his ministry—the focus changes to Paul as
prophet and spiritual leader. Finally, I offer some suggestions
about analogous functions of ministry today.

Paul the Apostle

Some might find it surprising to reflect that the only other
writer of a New Testament book whom we might be able to
consider in this way is John of Patmos, the author of the book
of Revelation. He is in fact the only other writer besides Paul
whose name we know with confidence. We are so accustomed
to the traditional or, in some cases, purported ascriptions of
the New Testament writings to figures from the apostolic age

George W. MacRae, Ph.D., is Stillman Professor of Roman Catholic
Theological Studies, Harvard Divinity School, Cambridge, Massachusetts.

that we do not always distinguish clearly those who, in their writings, genuinely reveal something of themselves, namely Paul and John of Patmos.

The underlying issue here is the nature of the New Testament books themselves, and I can do little more than allude to the question here. With the two exceptions mentioned, the New Testament books are either anonymous or pseudonymous; that is, they either do not tell us who wrote them or they lay claim to a personage of apostolic times as their author. For example, the four Gospels, the Acts of the Apostles, Hebrews, and the Johannine Epistles are all anonymous, although later tradition has ascribed them to specific authors. Some of the Pauline Epistles, such as the Pastorals, and some of the Catholic or General Epistles are widely believed to be pseudonymous, ascribed to Paul or Peter, for example, but not actually written by them. The latter practice may seem offensive to us as modern readers, who are sensitive to issues of forgery and plagiarism, but we must not project our sensitivities onto the ancient world. There is reason to believe that at least some works were written to honor the memory of revered figures and to perpetuate their teaching in new situations. In any case, the important point is that for most early Christian writers the proclamation of the gospel stands on its own, without the intrusion of an individual author's identity.

Paul and John of Patmos are the exceptions. Like Paul, only much more directly, John claims to be a prophet and the writer of prophecy (Revelation 1:3; 22:7–9, etc.). John's prophetic model may be Ezekiel; Paul's model is more difficult to identify. What the two have in common is that they are visionaries and their message rests on their own personal experience of Christ. For John, his whole book is an account of his visionary experience, narrated in the extravagant imagery of the apocalyptist and presented in the form of a letter. Paul in his various letters does not describe his visionary experiences in any detail, but only mentions them: his conversion involved "a revelation of Jesus Christ [Gal. 1:12]," and he was

100

the recipient of "visions and revelations of the Lord" in the "third heaven [2 Cor. 12:1–4]." For such persons as John and Paul the gospel message is very personal and must be communicated personally.

From the time of Adolf Deissmann's famous *Light from the Ancient East*[1] down to the most recent studies of ancient epistolography, much effort has been expended in New Testament scholarship to identify the models from Jewish and Greco-Roman culture for the Pauline letters. Yet, like the four Gospels, they remain somewhat elusive in terms of literary genre. They do not fit the contemporary models of either public or private letters, although they probably borrow from both. On the one hand, they are not strictly private letters, but are meant to be read to Christian congregations and perhaps even circulated (as the very probably pseudonymous letter to the Colossians explicitly states [Colossians 4:16]). Even the letter to Philemon is not private, being addressed to Philemon, Apphia, and Archippus as well as to "the church in your house [Philem. 1–2]." On the other hand, the letters are very personal, frequently dealing with Paul's close and sometimes intimate relationships with the communities he addresses.

Many readers of the Pauline letters have recognized the personal element but have found it less than warm. For them, Paul seems to be an extremely authoritarian figure who invokes his apostolic authority to issue commands to his churches in many areas of religious and moral life. It is true that he does not hesitate to claim authority, but a closer reading of the letters shows that he is not merely authoritarian. He often writes as a brother to his "brothers and sisters"—his favorite address to believers for whom the name Christians did not yet exist. He also writes as a father to his children (as in 1 Corinthians 4:14–15) and almost as a mother—at least as a nurse (1 Thessalonians 2:7). Paul's genuine tenderness is well brought out in his letter to what may have been his favorite community, the Philippians (see especially Philippians 1:3–11).

The picture of Paul as a warm friend of his churches should not, however, be taken as the whole picture. Taking his letters together, we find that he spends more time writing about his role as an apostle than as anything else. Indeed, he is preoccupied with this issue and extremely defensive about it. Obviously, he confronted others, including, of course, fellow Christians, who challenged his right to claim the title of apostle. It is indicative of the importance of this issue in the Pauline corpus that a great deal of recent writing on Paul's ministry has focused on his apostleship.[2]

In four of the letters—Romans, 1 and 2 Corinthians, and Galatians—Paul categorically identifies himself as an apostle in the opening epistolary greeting. In the last three of these letters, his right to the title is in question and he defends it vigorously; Romans is slightly different in that it is addressed to a church Paul does not know firsthand. If we put together some passages from these letters, we can see at least three conditions of Paul's understanding of apostle based on his own experience. First, an apostle is not self-proclaimed or elected by the church, but is called by God or by Christ to that role: "Paul, a servant of Jesus Christ, called to be an apostle, set apart for the gospel of God [Rom. 1:1]"; "Paul an apostle—not from men nor through man, but through Jesus Christ and God the Father [Gal. 1:1]." Second, an apostle must be one who has seen the risen Lord: "Am I not an apostle? Have I not seen Jesus our Lord? [1 Cor. 9:1]"; "Last of all, as to one untimely born, he appeared also to me. For I am the least of the apostles, unfit to be called an apostle, because I persecuted the church of God [1 Cor. 15:8–9]." Third, an apostle is one whose role is ratified, as it were, by the successful founding of Christian communities: "Are not you [Corinthians] my workmanship in the Lord? If to others I am not an apostle, at least I am to you; for you are the seal of my apostleship in the Lord [1 Cor. 9:1–2]." Taken individually, each of these conditions might be met by people other than apostles, but together they seem to define Paul's understanding of the title.

For Paul, an apostle is essentially a missionary preacher rather than the resident leader of an established church. "For Christ did not send me to baptize but to preach the gospel [1 Cor. 1:17]." The picture underlying a great many of Paul's references to his own activity is that of a fellow worker of God (1 Corinthians 3:9) who travels extensively, preaches the gospel of the saving death and resurrection of Christ, establishes new churches, revisits them, and leaves them eventually in the care of others (1 Corinthians 3–4). The fact that he fought so vigorously for recognition as an apostle in doing so perhaps indicates his awareness that a minister needs support and recognition on the part of the larger Christian community in order to be effective. Paul was independent but by no means a loner, such as were some of the classic prophets of the Old Testament. Although he does not normally associate prophetic language with his apostolic defense statements, he does so in Galatians 1:15, where he applies the prophetic calling of Jeremiah (cf. Jeremiah 1:5) to himself as an apostle: "When he who had set me apart before I was born, and had called me through his grace . . ." It is thus against the background of Paul's self-understanding as an apostle that we must turn to his role as a prophet.

Paul the Prophet

The extent to which Paul thought of himself as a Christian prophet is more difficult to determine because the evidence is indirect and allusive. That some early Christians thought of him in this way is not in doubt. Luke, in Acts 13:1, lists him along with Barnabas, Simeon Niger, Lucius of Cyrene, and Manaen of the Herodian court, some of whom are otherwise unknown, as among the "prophets and teachers" in the church of Antioch. To evaluate this identification, however, we must begin with a brief survey of early Christian notions of prophet.[3]

Unlike the case of apostle, in which the origins of the concept are, despite numerous scholarly theories, still shrouded in mystery, the notion of prophet is compounded by the major Old Testament background of the Israelite prophets plus the Greek prophets as interpreters of oracles and of poetic inspiration. Given the transition from the Hebrew designation of the prophet *(nabi)* to the Greek one *(prophētēs)*, which we may take to symbolize the broader transition from early Palestinian Christianity to the culture of the Greco-Roman world, one may not ignore either background in understanding prophets. The Israelite prophets were a rich, often colorful, and varied lot, and we cannot here survey all the Old Testament evidence, important as it is for shedding light on modern ministry.

The common denominator to all the ancient understandings of prophets is that their primary function is the sometimes awesome responsibility of proclaiming or interpreting the will of God to humanity. How they come by their insight into the divine will is not of primary significance. It may be by ecstatic experience, by divine revelation, or by reflection on the meaning of cult or of law or indeed of society. The important thing is that their vocation is to assure people that their message is indeed from God or the gods, and thus it may be portrayed as the deity communicating through them. In some cases, perhaps more true of the classic prophets of Israel than of the Greek interpreters of oracles, they actually speak in the name of the deity: "Thus says the Lord." I emphasize this point because we shall see that Christian prophets sometimes speak in the name of the Lord Jesus, and in so doing they are being traditional. And it is not surprising that, like their Old Testament counterparts, they are also sometimes controversial.

A majority of references to prophets in the New Testament are in fact to the prophets of the Old Testament, who are, of course, part of authoritative scripture for the early Christians. The role of these prophets emerges clearly in the New Testament use of them. They are people called by God to proclaim

God's word to God's people. Their functions are to exhort, to comfort, to threaten, to teach, and to advise—all in the name of God. In doing so they stand apart from the official, institutional structures of religion or society and thus enjoy a unique kind of freedom, although not always universal respect. To survey the role of the Old Testament prophets adequately, one would have to make distinctions among cultic prophets, associated with shrines; charismatic prophets, such as Elijah; court prophets, such as Nathan; and literary prophets, such as Amos or Isaiah. Of course, these distinctions are not always parallel or mutually exclusive. In post-Old Testament times, apocalyptic seers, such as Daniel (i.e., the fictitious personage to whom the book of Daniel was attributed), were also called prophets. Thus, the transmission of apocalyptic visions was admitted to the realm of prophetic functions. This last development influenced the prophetic understanding of John of Patmos, obviously, and enabled him to call his work prophecy and fit it into a line of tradition already well begun. Thus, one form of New Testament prophecy, the apocalyptic, is a direct descendant of older biblical models. In addition, against the Old Testament prophetic background, both John the Baptist and Jesus were sometimes interpreted as prophetic figures, but this branch of the tradition is not the main focus here.

Instead, we will examine those who may be called Christian prophets as in some sense leadership figures in the early church. Much of the evidence points to the origin of the Christian prophets as charismatic figures who were unconnected with any church structure of an official kind. They did, however, apparently become somewhat institutionalized, at least by the time of the *Didache,* an important church order document dating perhaps from about 100 C.E. There we find that prophets are itinerant, authoritative leaders (who may choose to settle down, *Didache* 13.1), whose actual functions are not spelled out in detail. When they assume leadership in worship, they are not to be challenged (10.7). Whether or what they preach, and one assumes preaching is their main function, we are not told. For the *Didache*, apostles and prophets seem virtually identical in their roles (11.3–6). But prophets seem also to be inherently objects of legitimate suspicion. If they seek personal gain, or even if they remain too long, living off the local community, they are to be rejected (11.5–6, 9, 12). Apparently, early Christian prophets were easy to imitate, perhaps because they were autonomous; there are frequent warnings against false prophets in the *Didache* and in the New Testament (e.g., Matthew 7:15; Mark 13:22; Acts 13:6; 2 Peter 2:1; 1 John 4:1; *Didache* 11.5–6).

It is Luke, however temporally remote his evidence is, who provides examples of numerous prophets in the churches in the Acts of the Apostles. For one thing, he portrays a certain prophet from Jerusalem named Agabus predicting a great famine over all the Mediterranean world in the time of the Emperor Claudius (Acts 11:28). Later in the narrative (21:10–11), Agabus predicts the arrest of Paul and his being handed over to the gentiles. Prediction of future events was not the essence of biblical prophecy at any period, but in the popular mind then as now such soothsaying powers were associated with prophets, and this may be what Luke portrays in Acts. Agabus is no mere soothsayer for Luke, however; it is by virtue of the Holy Spirit, for whom Agabus is a spokesman, that the future is made known in both cases. Prophetic activity as Acts depicts it was not necessarily the prerogative of an elite and certainly not an authoritative office in the church. I have already mentioned the group of prophets at Antioch (Acts 13:1); at Caesarea, where Agabus is last seen, we are told of the four maiden daughters of Philip the evangelist who prophesy (21:9). But despite the prominence of prophets in Acts, there does not emerge a clear picture of what is their function in the church.

To get a somewhat clearer focus on prophets in early, predominantly gentile Christian communities, we must turn to Paul and specifically to 1 Corinthians 14, which is virtually the only informative passage. Already in 1 Corinthians 12:10 and

106

28, Paul has listed prophecy or prophets among the particularized gifts of the Holy Spirit in the body of Christ (cf. 1 Corinthians 13:2, 9). In chapter 14, presumably in response to a specific question of the Corinthian Christians, he ventures on the sensitive ground of evaluating comparatively the gifts of prophecy and speaking in tongues. His argument and his solution are well known. Both gifts are exercised in the context of the public worship of the community. Speaking in tongues, however, because it is essentially unintelligible (although it may be interpreted) and therefore addressed privately to God, "edifies," that is, builds up, the (faith of) the individual rather than the community. And for that reason, it is, in Paul's view, of lesser value than prophecy, which is of its nature intelligible (thus not essentially ecstatic) and a contribution to the building up of the community as such, including its marginal or even backsliding members (cf. 14:16). The only limitation Paul recommends is that it be practiced in an orderly fashion—order being one of his main concerns in worship (see also chapter 11)—and this very limitation suggests that prophecy could be abused in something like an ecstatic way unless kept under control.

The questions remain: What is Christian prophecy? And who are the prophets? The second question is easy to answer, but the answer is not entirely satisfactory. According to 1 Corinthians 12 and 14, prophets are any members of the community who have the gift of prophecy. One may have the gift; one may also aspire to and even strive to have it. What is less than satisfying is that Paul provides only one criterion for discerning this gift: the hardly negligible criterion of building up the community rather than the individual as such. Vague or unspecific as it may appear, this criterion is of major importance for Paul's entire understanding of Christian existence. For him, the Christian is one who lives for others, not for himself or herself in the first place. Such a measure is all the more applicable to those who would be leaders of the community in worship or elsewhere.

The first of the two questions—What is Christian prophecy according to 1 Corinthians 14?—must be answered largely by inference. Prophecy is clearly some kind of rationally intelligible hortatory preaching—which, one might observe, is what preaching is generally expected to be, then as now. One who prophesies speaks to people "for their upbuilding and encouragement and consolation [14:3]." To be more precise about the content of prophetic preaching in Corinth, one must ask yet another question.

Did Paul consider himself a prophet? He certainly thought of himself as an apostle and as one favored with the gift of speaking in tongues (14:18). Did he also have the gift of prophecy? One is inclined almost a priori to infer that he did, since he urges the Corinthians to strive for this gift, and since in general he urges them to become imitators of him (cf. 1 Corinthians 11:1). But one does not have to remain at this theoretical level of inference. In such verses as 1 Corinthians 14:6 and 19, he speaks in the first person of delivering prophecy to the assembly. If these are more than just generic examples using the first person—and I think that they are more—then they imply that Paul practices the gift of prophecy himself when he worships with the community.

As he comes to the conclusion of his long argument about the superiority of prophecy over tongues in public worship, he makes what I take to be a revealing statement: "If any one thinks that he is a prophet, or spiritual, he should acknowledge that what I am writing to you is a command of the Lord [1 Cor. 14:37."⁴ Of course, we know of no command of Jesus regulating good order in Christian worship, and there is unlikely to have been one. The principle underlying this statement is the ancient one of like being known by like. The Christian prophet in Corinth will recognize that Paul's instruction on worship is itself an example of Christian prophecy. But according to this statement, how does the prophet recognize it as prophecy? Because it is presented as coming from Jesus himself. The Christian prophet, like the prophets of the Old Testament, proclaims the will of God, in this case doubtless the will of Jesus, to his people, and does so in the words of Jesus himself. The ultimate root of this motivation or conviction, found in personal experience of Jesus, is inaccessible to us. But the purpose of prophecy is the upbuilding and encouragement and consolation of the church.

Modern biblical scholarship is familiar with the theory elaborated by Ernst Käsemann that it was the distinctive role of Christian prophets to formulate sayings of the Lord—many of them simply attributed to Jesus in accounts of his lifetime—to suit new situations and crises in the life of the churches.[5] Käsemann even identified the form of such sayings as what he called "sentences of holy law." His thesis has come under a good deal of criticism in its particulars,[6] but its basic thrust may well be valid and to some extent confirmed by Paul in 1 Corinthians 14:37. This is to say that the distinctively prophetic feature of early Christian hortatory preaching was the communication in terms of sayings of the Lord of the Lord's will for new situations in the life of the church.

Paul the Spiritual Leader

The second part of the title of this essay describes Paul as spiritual leader. Perhaps one notes a sort of jarring modern ring to this expression; it is hardly a Pauline term. In fact, I chose it because it is modern but may also lead us to some real considerations of Paul's understanding of his own ministry. The problem at the outset is that it is not clear how or to what extent Paul as spiritual leader differs from Paul as prophet. In what follows I shall point out how the two are closely related, without trying to modernize Paul unduly. Again, 1 Corinthians is the main source.

The issue of who was a "spiritual person" apparently was one of the main problems at Corinth. Some members of the Corinthian community certainly claimed this prerogative for themselves, as is implied at several points in 1 Corinthians, such as 3:1. In all probability, the Corinthian Christians did not derive this self-understanding merely from their Greco-Roman background. In fact, the term spiritual *(pneumatikos)* was rather uncommon as a designation of those who were outside of Christian circles at this period. And for Christians, it meant not simply people who were dominated by spirit as opposed to the material or the physical, but people in relation to the Spirit of God. In confronting the Corinthians, Paul does not so much challenge the understanding of the claim to be spiritual as question the understanding of what God's Spirit implies for human life and conduct. He can, of course, distinguish the "spirit of the world" from the "Spirit which is from God [1 Cor. 2:12]," but it is the latter that is more problematic for the Corinthians. For Paul, being suffused by the Spirit of God demands a process of discernment of spirits lest the believer confuse God's Spirit with a lesser one, associated purely with human preferences (1 Corinthians 12:4–11).

The question is whether or not Paul understood his role over against the Corinthians as that of a Spirit-filled person instructing people who thought of themselves as spiritual—and what form this instruction took. Perhaps the best example is in the long and complex seventh chapter of 1 Corinthians. Here Paul answers questions of the church regarding the nature and obligations of marriage and celibacy as alternative ways of life. It is not my purpose to survey the issues or the answers, which are well known, but rather the attitude of the writer. The chapter deals seriatim with a number of questions: the exercise of marital rights, marriage itself, the prohibition of divorce, an exception to this in "mixed" marriages, stability of life, the value of celibacy, the situation of the engaged, and the rights of widows. These were sensitive issues in the society of Paul's day, as they have been throughout history. In only one case can he appeal to a saying of the Lord (Jesus), that of the prohibition of divorce (1 Corinthians 7:10–11; cf. Mark 10:11–12 and parallel). In all other cases he is, as it were, on his own; for example, 1 Corinthians 7:25: "I have no command of the Lord, but I give my opinion as one who by the Lord's mercy is trustworthy." Yet his ultimate qualification for all this teaching rests not on himself or his apostolic authority, but on his role as a spiritual leader. This is expressed most clearly in the last verse of the chapter (7:40, TEV): "And I think that I too have God's Spirit." His subtle assertion that he "too" has the Spirit of God is a reminder to the Corinthians, who think of themselves as spiritual, that their pretensions must not be exclusive.

Yet it is noteworthy that in chapter 7, Paul is doing something analogous to what he does in chapter 14, namely, laying down instructions for the church in situations not envisioned by the ministry of Jesus himself, in the latter case involving regulations for worship and in the former, rules for personal life. In the latter case, he appeals, at least implicitly, to his role as prophet, in the former, to his role as one who has the Spirit of God. The reader can only be struck by the similarity of the situations and the conclusion that, for Paul, one who is imbued with the Spirit is a prophet if he or she builds up the community, and certainly a prophet is one who is imbued with the Spirit. Ultimately, Paul as spiritual leader and Paul as prophet are one. What holds both situations together is that he interprets the will of the Lord for new situations in the life of the church. The identity of these functions is confirmed by the language of 1 Corinthians 14:37: "If any one thinks that he is a prophet, or spiritual, he should acknowledge that what I am writing to you is a command of the Lord."

Prophecy and Prophetic Ministry

Can one legitimately draw conclusions for the modern situation from this Pauline understanding of ministry as prophecy and what we have called spiritual leadership? The answer must obviously be: only with caution, caution because of the immense distance between the Pauline ministry and the modern ministry in time, in culture, and in basic understanding.

Yet we must ask the question; otherwise, the study of Pauline ministry is of merely antiquarian interest. Rather than draw out detailed applications for an understanding of Christian ministry today, I should like to deal with two provocative conclusions from an examination of the texts, with the full awareness that much more needs ultimately to be said.

First, in what sense is ministry properly regarded as prophetic? One answer to this question has not been dealt with in this essay: the one that is based more or less exclusively on the role of the principal prophets of the Old Testament. It is that of speaking out against the establishment, political or religious, in the name of God and God's people whenever the establishment has "evolved" to the stage of preserving itself rather than defending the needs of God's people. There have always been times when this has been a proper ministerial role, but it is a lonely road and a difficult one. It is not precisely the one to which this essay is addressed; yet it is a vital one.

Instead, I should like to concentrate on prophecy and prophetic ministry, as concerned with interpreting the will of God for the present time. If this were the sole definition of ministry, it would sound like sheer arrogance. Yet it is an essential part of that ministry. If the minister is not called forth from the community for this task, what exactly is his or her primary function? The charge may indeed seem overwhelming. It implies that the minister is sufficiently informed biblically, theologically, and ethically, is perceptive, is sensitive, is prayerful, is humble enough, to speak for God in new situations. The dangers of individualism or idiosyncrasy are obvious, and the only check on them is conscious adherence to the church, however narrowly or broadly this is conceived. Intellectual or moral isolation is the principal peril. Paul himself, an independent thinker by many reckonings, could say: "Whether then it was I or they, so we preach and so you believed [1 Cor. 15:11]." No matter how lonely the burden of the ministry may seem, it need never be an isolated one.

The second conclusion has more to do with the cultural difference between the first century and the waning twentieth. Paul did not conceive of the basic Christian attitudes as individual responses to God or to Christ. For him, God's relationship was with God's people, whether Israel or the Christian church, not with a mere collection of individuals. Paul's primary metaphor for the people whom God redeemed in Christ was that of the body of Christ, not individual believers. In contrast, modern Christians, heirs of the systematic individualism of the Enlightenment, tend inevitably to conceive of the biblical message as being addressed to them as individuals. To the extent that spirituality is thought of exclusively in individual terms, ministry as spiritual leadership becomes a matter of the care of souls on a one-to-one basis. Today the situation is compounded by the triumph of individual psychology in our culture. For some, a ministry of spiritual leadership becomes almost indistinguishable from a ministry of psychological counseling in a religious setting. Some knowledge of psychology is an indispensable tool for the minister, of course, and nothing said here is meant to deny it. But if we are to learn something from Paul's prophetic and spiritual ministry, it may be that ministry is also the formation and leadership of Christian communities that need above all to hear the word of God addressing them in their own situations.

There need be no opposition between the individual and the community. Many of Paul's prophetic instructions to his churches concern things that ultimately have to be implemented by individuals. The difference is that, for Paul, the Christian individual is in large measure defined by belonging to the Christian community, sharing in its blessings and its responsibilities, measuring involvement in terms of others and not merely of self. Paul's prophetic ministry is a salutary reminder of this in an age of almost excessive individualism.

CHAPTER 6

The Passion of God and the
Prophetic Task of Pastoral Ministry

Daniel L. Migliore

THE "PASSION OF GOD" HAS BECOME A CENTRAL SYMBOL IN
contemporary theology. As perhaps few other symbols of
Christian faith, it speaks compellingly to many people in our
time.

The Passion of God and Human Apathy

Although the highly paradoxical claim that "only the suffering God can help" is usually associated with the prison writings of Dietrich Bonhoeffer, variations on this motif may be
found in virtually every major theological movement of recent
years. The trinitarian theologies of Jürgen Moltmann and
Eberhard Jüngel, the liberation theologies of Gustavo Gutiérrez and Jon Sobrino, the narrative political theology of Johann
Baptist Metz, the feminist political theology of Dorothee
Soelle, the black theology of James Cone, the process the-

Daniel L. Migliore, Ph.D., is professor of systematic theology at Princeton Theological Seminary, Princeton, New Jersey.

ology of John Cobb, the mystical theology of Hans Urs von Balthasar—all give prominent place to the theme of the passion of God.

But like all central symbols of Christian faith, the passion of God carries not just one meaning, but a surplus of meanings. Each of the theologians or theological schools I have mentioned interprets this symbol in a distinctive way. Some of these interpretations are complementary; others appear to be in conflict with one another. In particular, two meanings of the passion of God stand out in contemporary theology. On the one hand, the passion of God expresses God's partisanship for the poor, God's advocacy of justice for the weak and the oppressed. I will call this the *prophetic* understanding of the passion of God because it wants to eliminate all suffering and calls attention to God's uncompromising judgment on and resistance to evil. On the other hand, the passion of God refers to God's own suffering love in solidarity with the afflicted, God's own freely accepted experience of rejection and affliction in company with all groaning creatures. I will call this the *pastoral* understanding of the passion of God. In this view, the passion of God expresses the ultimate mystery of the divine agape by which we are reconciled with God and with one another. Although the passion of God stands in judgment on all unjust suffering, it also reveals that suffering can be redemptive when it arises out of the freedom of love.

My purpose in this essay is to show that these two meanings of the passion of God are interdependent rather than mutually exclusive. They must be held together and allowed to correct and enrich each other if we are to be responsible to the biblical witness and if our ministry today is to have integrity and credibility. My argument will be developed in several steps. First, since our understanding of God and our understanding of ourselves are always intertwined, I shall briefly describe our present culture of apathy and the failure of our traditional images of God to challenge this apathy. Second, I shall contend that the biblical witness to the passion of God struggles against our apathy-producing idols of power and summons us both to pastoral compassion and to prophetic resistance. In the third and fourth sections, I shall explore more fully the prophetic task of pastoral ministry and the pastoral task of prophetic ministry, each in the light of the passion of God.

The Present Culture of Apathy

We begin where John Calvin began in his *Institutes:* with the claim that understandings of God and of ourselves are reciprocally related.[1] This axiom of theological reflection points to the need for every theology to offer some preliminary description or diagnosis of the cultural situation of its time if it is to speak of God responsibly and understandably.

I want to propose, then, that an adequate theological analysis of the experience of many people today is not exhausted by such familiar theological descriptions of the human condition as guilt, pride, angst, radical dependency, and the like, descriptions that have achieved classic status in the theologies of the Reformation and more recently in neoorthodox theology. Stated positively, the deadly spiritual disease of our time that is overlooked by these familiar theological categories is apathy. *It is only in conjunction with a heightened awareness of our apathetic human condition that we can begin to grasp the significance of the image of the passion of God.*

As commonly used, the word passion has the dual meanings of a strong emotion and of an experience of suffering. We speak of an intense desire as a passion, but we also speak of a history of suffering, and in particular of the suffering that Jesus endured, as a passion. Correspondingly, the word apathy has the dual meanings of an absence of feeling and of a state of inability to be affected by others. Apathy in both of these senses is an entirely understandable human response to a century of disillusionment and horror: two world wars, countless brutal regional wars, the holocaust of six million Jews in Europe, the staggering ecological costs of industrial

116

and technological development, and the growing threat of the nuclear self-annihilation of the human race. Contra Karl Marx, it is not religion but apathy that is the opium we administer to ourselves to escape the all-too-painful facts of world, national, or personal history.

Apathy goes to the root of our moral and spiritual crisis today. It leads to a contraction of the religious life to the private zone of existence and to a failure of moral nerve in the public arena. Apathy is the loss of ability to feel indignant at the work of evil in our lives and in the lives of others. It is the absence of outrage against injustice. It is the erosion of ability to commit oneself to important causes, to care deeply about other people, and to take risks in the struggle against every form of human bondage. Apathy says: "What's the use? Nothing ever changes. We must simply get accustomed to the way things are. Peace, justice, and human wholeness are only empty ideals that have no chance against such hard realities as the poverty and hunger that stalk the Third World or the global arms race that threatens the very survival of life on our planet." Thus, apathy and resignation conquer compassion and courage, and we become incredibly ingenious in explaining how suffering—usually the suffering of others—is not so bad after all. One can learn to live with it, once one discovers what "fix" (whether drugs, alcohol, consumerism, or absorption in work or leisure) produces the desired apathetic condition.

The causes and symptoms of apathy are complex. In the following comments I can do little more than touch the surface of the widespread experience of apathy and desensitization.

1. Apathy grows in direct proportion to the feeling of being controlled by events, institutions, and people who render us utterly helpless. Apathy triumphs where people think of themselves as mere pawns of fate or chance or of power that is unresponsive and is exercised in arbitrary and dominative ways. The persistent experience of manipulative or coercive

power, or the threat of such power, in family relations, in the workplace, or in an entire social system makes people apathetic.

2. Although the condition of apathetic humanity is found in every society today, whether developed or undeveloped, the underlying reasons are diverse. Apathy is fostered in the Third World by the experience of centuries of oppression and bondage. The birth of new hope in such situations is, unfortunately, made still more difficult by the attitudes of many people in the First World who refuse to see the need and promise of movements of social transformation in poor countries and who feel more comfortable with the pervasive apathy that often attends poverty, tyranny, and rule by terror. It is, however, not the apathy of people in the Third World, but of people in the First and Second Worlds, in developed societies both East and West, that must be the primary object of our reflection. In developed societies, apathy is associated not with poverty, but with satiation and loss of meaning. Bureaucratization, depersonalization, and a vague sense of powerlessness to do anything that might make a real difference contribute to the condition of apathy in economically advanced societies.

3. Apathy is promoted by the pervasive disconnection from concrete suffering—both the suffering of others and of one's own—that has become an ideal in modern society. A life entirely free of any suffering is the goal we set for ourselves and for our children. The dark side of life is systematically excluded, or is something to be experienced only secondhand. Dorothee Soelle describes this situation as follows: "One learns about the suffering of others only indirectly—one sees starving children on TV—and this kind of relationship to the suffering of others is characteristic of our entire perception. We seldom experience even the suffering and death of friends and relatives physically and directly."[2]

118

4. Apathy is not only destructive in its effect on others, depriving them of the help and companionship that they need, but also profoundly self-destructive. Although apathy often begins in a denial of the suffering of others—an averting of one's eyes from the needs of the afflicted neighbors and a closing of one's ears to their cries—the cost that the apathetic self has to pay is high. As Soelle writes:

> One wonders what will become of a society in which certain forms of suffering are avoided gratuitously, in keeping with middle-class ideals. I have in mind a society in which: a marriage that is perceived as unbearable quickly and smoothly ends in divorce; after divorce no scars remain; relationships between generations are dissolved as quickly as possible, without a struggle, without a trace; periods of mourning are 'sensibly' short; with haste the handicapped and sick are removed from the house and the dead from the mind. If changing marriage partners happens as readily as trading in an old car on a new one, then the experiences that one had in the unsuccessful relationship remain unproductive. From suffering nothing is learned and nothing is to be learned.[3]

The point is that as we make ourselves indifferent to the afflictions of others, we become increasingly insensitive to our own pain. Human beings are created by God for life in relationship, for life in community. When we deny our bond with others, we also deny ourselves. If we anesthetize our feeling of kinship, we are in grave danger of losing all feeling whatever.

5. Thus, apathy moves in a vicious circle. It may begin with indifference to the suffering of others, but this eventually contributes to the evasion and denial of our own afflictions, our own need for help, liberation, and transformation. And the vicious circle continues. Our denial of our real human interdependence, our own personal tragedies, our own need of liberation from the forces of this world that hold us in bondage further desensitizes us to the real suffering of others.

"Whoever deals with his personal suffering only in the way our society has taught him—through illusion, minimization, suppression, apathy—will deal with societal suffering in the same way."[4]

6. Within this demonic and all-encompassing circle of apathy, traditional ways of thinking and speaking of God seem less a challenge to than a confirmation of the pattern of life we have called apathetic. If God is routinely called omnipotent, this connotes for many people total control over others, the exercise of complete, unilateral, and even coercive power. Omnipotence then becomes synonymous with the godalmightiness that Karl Barth once described as an attribute of Satan rather than of the true God who became a servant for our sake. When omnipotence is understood as godalmightiness, God is nothing more than the religious projection of those forces of the world that terrify us and render us helpless and apathetic. Only a God who exercises power in a way altogether different from coercive control is able to help us out of our apathy. In this sense, Bonhoeffer was right: "Only a suffering God can help."

Similarly, if God is said to be pure activity and in no way receptive, if God is supremely incapable of being affected by what happens in the world, blissfully untouched by its sufferings, if it is demeaning and naive to speak of God as passionate advocate of justice and peace in the creation, then again God becomes nothing more than a religious projection of that safety and invulnerability of indifference that we elect in our apathetic lives. Belief in an apathetic God serves only to sanction and reinforce our own socially destructive and self-destructive apathy. God as the ideal of invulnerability and of a life free from suffering helps to destroy the ability of people to love, to risk relationship, and to experience deeply the joy and pain of life in community.

Thus, our explicit or implicit images of God as absolute monarch or distant patriarch, as invulnerable and untouchable, enter into secret alliance with a dehumanizing way of life. Knowledge of God and knowledge of ourselves are indeed bound inseparably together. A culture in which power is equated with domination over others and in which people quietly slide into apathy sees itself reflected in a deity that controls everything but is inwardly affected by nothing.

If the condition of apathy is to be overcome, a necessary first step is the discovery of a language that exposes our condition and points us in a radically different direction. Precisely that is the aim of the bold and disturbing language of the passion of God.

Prophetic and Pastoral Dimensions of God's Passion

Still influential descriptions of God characterize the deity as exclusively active, never passive, as only giver and never receiver of anything from the world, as possessor of every conceivable perfection and hence incapable of any passion, as being in total control and never experiencing weakness. In contrast to such a picture of God, *the biblical witness proclaims a God who is the supremely passionate advocate of justice and whose power is defined precisely by the freedom to undergo passion for others.*

If anything is clear about the God of the Bible, it is that this God is not in any sense apathetic. Abraham Heschel goes to the heart of the matter by speaking of the "pathos" of the God of the prophets.[5] What Heschel calls the pathos of God includes both meanings of divine passion that were distinguished earlier. Because God is understood as the covenant God who is the relentless advocate of justice for the poor, the prophets declare the utter irreconcilability of faithfulness to God and any compliance with exploitation and injustice. At the same time, God is more than advocate; God is personally affected by the suffering of people, takes up their suffering and makes it God's own. Far from being a sign of ineffec-

121

tiveness, this divine compassion is a manifestation of redemptive strength that will finally be victorious over all evil.

The prophets value obedience to God's will and social transformation over loyalty to the king and social stability. In confrontation with kings and the royal ideology, the prophets proclaim God's command for justice in the common life as an essential part of faithfulness to the covenant God. As God's jealousy prohibits every form of idolatry, so God's anger is aroused by every abuse of power. Isaiah declares that God looks for justice and finds instead bloodshed (Isaiah 5:7). Amos insists that God despises feasts and solemn assemblies and desires instead that justice roll down like waters and righteousness like an everflowing stream (Amos 5:21–24). The God of the prophets is a passionate God, however tasteless this depiction may appear to a pseudosophisticated modern mentality that considers itself superior to all such anthropomorphisms and finds it easier to relate to a God who reflects its own apathy.

But the prophets also see God as deeply affected by the disobedience of the people and by their suffering. God not only acts, but also suffers. How else can one interpret the words of Hosea portraying the tender parental compassion of Yahweh? "How can I give you up, O Ephraim! . . . My heart recoils within me, my compassion grows warm and tender. I will not execute my fierce anger, I will not again destroy Ephraim; for I am God and not man, the Holy One in your midst, and I will not come to destroy [Hos. 11:8–9]." In the writings of Isaiah, Jeremiah, and Hosea, God laments over what is happening to people. These lamentations arise out of God's wounded love that created humanity free and desires love and faithfulness in response to the divine love. God freely becomes vulnerable to the rejection and the afflictions of people. God grieves in their grief and goes into exile in their exile. Thus, for the prophets, God is both the source of protest against evil and suffering and the source of consolation and empowerment that comes from God's own suffering in solidarity with the afflicted. Prophetic resistance and pastoral companionship are woven together tightly in the passion of God.

Jesus stands in this bold prophetic tradition, and the two sides of the passion of God that are characteristic of the prophets are present in a decisive way in the gospel story. The life, death, and resurrection of Jesus is the supreme expression of the passion of God for fullness of life, justice, and peace in all the creation. The ministry of Jesus is a ministry of passionate advocacy of God's coming kingdom. Jesus disturbs and liberates as he proclaims and enacts God's acceptance of sinners, the poor, and the outcast. He concretely announces forgiveness of sinners, reconciliation among enemies, and justice for the poor and thereby summons all to repentance and renewal of life. But the gospel story presents Jesus not only as actor, but also as sufferer; not only as judge, but also as the one judged in our place; not only as one who protests against evil in God's creation, but also as one who freely and redemptively suffers in and for all suffering creatures.

The deepest intention of the later trinitarian doctrine of the church is to take account of the divine passion in our understanding of the reality of God.[6] Trinitarian doctrine brings to expression the biblical proclamation that the sovereign God is active, suffering, transforming love. God is not absolute, authoritarian power, but the power of self-giving, other-affirming, community-forming love. The God of the gospel is the God who is in relationship, the God who can freely suffer with and for another and thus can love, the God of open friendship and inclusive community. The biblical witness and its compressed expression in trinitarian doctrine see God not as the supreme power of control and domination over others, but as the power that creates a community of free people because it is the power of suffering, liberating love. Every form of theological tyranny and patriarchy distorts this revolutionary trinitarian understanding of God.

In contemporary theology and ministry, there is a tendency

to separate what is united in the biblical witness and in the classic trinitarian faith of the church. What we have called the prophetic and pastoral dimensions of the passion of God in Jesus Christ are allowed to fall apart, and the result is that we become prophetic activists with no pastoral compassion, on the one hand, or caretakers of souls with no prophetic vision or commitment, on the other. Each of these polarized forms of ministry simply contributes to our apathetic condition.

This polarization is evident, for example, in the individualistic understandings of the passion and resurrection of Jesus that are typical of the piety of many North American Christians. Emptied of all critical prophetic meaning, the message of the cross is easily taken to support resignation to conditions of injustice and exploitation. In the past, this meant providing legitimacy, at least indirectly and sometimes quite directly, to the institution of slavery. In the present, it means showing the compatibility of the gospel with structures of injustice affecting women and other marginalized groups in society. A theology and ministry that is faithful to the biblical witness, however, will always discern in the story of the passion of God a dangerous rather than a domesticating memory. The dangerous memory of the passion of God "breaks the grip of the prevailing consciousness."[7] It shatters all idols of power because it sees God in solidarity with the poor and all who suffer and yearn for justice. Memory of the passion of God holds fast to the incongruity between the will of God and the disorder of our personal lives and of our social structures. Properly understood, the passion of God will always heighten our awareness of the divine judgment on present injustice rather than creating a spirit of resignation. If God is present among us in radical contradiction and protest as well as in forgiveness and promise, then those who recall this disturbing presence of God must themselves struggle against all conditions of injustice and resist oppression wherever it exists. This is the heart of the prophetic retrieval of the meaning of the passion of God: that suffering caused by injustice and oppression must be opposed.

But the biblical unity of the prophetic and pastoral dimensions of the passion of God can also be lost if the prophetic protest against injustice uncritically adopts the prevailing understanding and exercise of power as power that seeks control and domination. In the gospel story, God in Christ not only protests against a sinful misuse of power, but also puts into practice a new exercise of power as agapic love. The future of prophetic theology and ministry that intend to stand within the biblical tradition depends on a radical redefinition of the power of God and of what constitutes true human power. If the passion of God is integral to the power of God, then suffering, if freely assumed for the sake of others and set within an inclusive redemptive purpose, is alien neither to God nor to true humanity. This is the heart of the pastoral retrieval of the meaning of the passion of God: that under certain conditions, suffering can help to make us more human.

Prophetic and Pastoral Ministry and the Sacraments

If my reflections to this point have been sound, it follows that *in the light of the passion of God, pastoral ministry must be prophetic.* This is simply to say that pastoral ministry must never become a means of inculcating attitudes of submission and resignation to evil in personal or social existence. Protest against experienced evil and injustice is a legitimate and even necessary element in all Christian life and in all authentic pastoral ministry. If our ministry is guided by the prophetic spirit of resistance and by the all-transforming Spirit of Christ, we will refuse to deny, evade, or adjust to the reality of evil in the world.

On Easter Sunday morning in 1984, a group of angry, unemployed steelworkers from the economically devastated Monongahela Valley disrupted the worship service at Shadyside Presbyterian Church in Pittsburgh. They confronted the congregation, which has a sizable endowment, with the physical needs of the families of the jobless. Beyond this, they protested the policies of the big steel companies and powerful banks—and their churchgoing executive officers—of investing in overseas mills, where labor is considerably cheaper, rather than in local steel mills. Similar demonstrations have continued on Sunday mornings at other prominent churches in the Pittsburgh area.

The tactics of the protestors were widely criticized by many church members and by much of the mass media. Such criticism was predictable and perhaps in part justifiable. The larger questions, however, are whether the voices of protest have any place in the church and how, after the initial shock, churches should respond to a challenge of this sort. Will the pastors and members of these churches seek primarily to secure their property and their rights against this "invasion" of demonstrators? Or will they be open to discern a possible correspondence between the prophetic tradition of the Bible and the action of these steelworkers and their families who are bearing a disproportionate share of the burden of complex social and economic change?

Although pastoral ministry is many-sided, surely one of its tasks is to help people to identify and oppose the evil that is afflicting them and others. Unfortunately, we often shrink from this responsibility. Just as we are inclined rather prematurely to make acceptance of death the norm of our counseling with the dying, so we are inclined to rush to the acceptance of systemic unemployment or other social evils. In this way, the anguished cries of people are silenced or muted. Pastoral ministry should give people permission to protest against evil rather than seek to bring about quick and easy accommodation to it. The message of reconciliation must not be turned into a policy of costless reconcilism. Jesus' own "cry of dereliction" stands in the way of this, for it is the authorization given by the crucified one to all who are afflicted to join the great

126

tradition of lament of prophets and psalmists in registering a mighty protest against the outrageous power of evil and suffering in the world.

Once we begin to take seriously the biblical tradition of prophetic protest and its ultimate rootage in the passion of God decisively made known in Jesus Christ, the prophetic dimensions of all the central acts of pastoral ministry become evident. Prayer, so basic to all Christian life and pastoral ministry, is the most obvious case in point. Whenever prayer is practiced, an unsettling, even explosive factor is introduced into human life. In the first three petitions of the Lord's Prayer, we ask that God's name be hallowed, that God's kingdom come, and that God's will be done on earth as in heaven. These petitions are far removed from all privatistic religion. They open us to world-encompassing concerns: to zeal for the honor of God and passion for the establishment of justice and peace everywhere. Praying the Lord's Prayer does not commit us to a particular political program, but it does turn us in a particular political direction. It envisions nothing less than the renewal of the entire earth.

Or again, when we pray for leaders who are in authority over us, we are not resigning ourselves unconditionally to their wills. On the contrary, by praying for them, we acknowledge that they are *not* the final authority, that they stand under a higher authority to which both they and we are responsible. We acknowledge, in other words, that they are in need of help and guidance from beyond themselves, and hence our prayer for them declares their authority to be relative, fallible, and provisional. In the prophetic biblical tradition, prayer is always potentially an act of political resistance. Totalitarian regimes recognize this and attempt either to regulate prayer or to proscribe it. As long as prayer is in the name of Jesus, who was crucified by the established authorities and who cried out in abandonment on the cross, it will remain an event by which not only personal, but also social and political protest against evil is given voice and thus kept alive.

There is also an unmistakable prophetic dimension in the celebration of the sacraments. The sacrament of baptism is the sacrament of our solidarity with Jesus in his dying and hence our solidarity with all his brothers and sisters for whom he died and rose again. Baptism is our induction into the community of Christ, in which old barriers of class, race, and sex are broken down and mutual respect and friendship are built up. The apostle Paul may be repeating an ancient Christian baptismal formula when he declares that in Christ "there is neither Jew nor Greek, there is neither slave nor free, there is neither male nor female [Gal. 3:28]." The new community into which we enter by baptism into Christ includes all manner of people and binds us together both in suffering and in hope. The meaning of baptism surely has some bearing on the recent demonstrations of steelworkers in the Pittsburgh churches. According to one newspaper report, the leaders of one congregation, flanked by local police, blocked the entryway to the church as protestors approached. In another report, one of the protestors is quoted as saying, "We are Christians too."[8] Should not our baptism vividly remind us of our solidarity in Christ with all who groan under the powers of sin and death and who seek God's new order?

If baptism is the sacrament of Christian solidarity, the Lord's Supper is the sacrament of Christian sharing. In the Lord's Supper, we celebrate that event in which the very life of God is shared freely with us, and we are called to share ourselves and our resources with others. At this table all are fed. Participation in the sacrament of the Lord's Supper should motivate action on behalf of the hungry of the world. And this begins with the needy neighbor closest to us. All people need to be fed with the Word who is the bread of life, but all people also need to be fed with the bread that is the physical necessity of life. The Lord's Supper is a proclamation of the passion of God for life, justice, freedom, and peace, and it summons us to prophetic Christian witness and service.

I have stressed the prophetic aspects of prayer and sacraments. At the heart of the church's ministry is the proclamation of the gospel that Jesus Christ is Lord. This is both a religious and a political statement, since it expresses our ultimate allegiance and calls into question every other claimant to authority. No cherished custom or familiar way of life can be allowed to compete with the trust and loyalty that we may properly give to Christ alone. Moreover, when the gospel is expounded as the message of salvation by grace alone through faith, this message has profound implications for our ordering of our common life and for our social and political priorities. The foundation of human worth and dignity is in God's affirmation of us as men and women created in the divine image and redeemed for fellowship with God and with one another. We are "somebodies" not because of what we have inherited or what we produce or what we consume, but because of what we are and are to become by God's grace. That always has been and always will be the Christian foundation of human dignity and human rights. In short, the gospel of God's sovereign love is a message generative of prophetic political vision and transformative action so long as the church does not hide its light under a bushel of domesticating and privatizing interpretations.

Reflections such as these might set the context for a creative response of the Shadyside church and other churches to the cries and protests of suffering people. Surely as Christians we must get beyond the self-defensive impulse to forbid the protestors from entering the church, to call the police, and to invoke the rights of private property. Has not the liturgy of Israel and of the church always given people language and voice to express their deepest sufferings and hopes, a language and a voice without which they would be mute or could express themselves only in acts of desperation? Is it not then altogether appropriate to begin to work together on the pain of the unemployed steelworkers in the liturgy of the people of God, and what more appropriate time than Easter morning?

Perhaps these questions, together with our brief survey of

the central acts of pastoral ministry—prayer, sacraments, and proclamation—will help to clarify what is meant by saying that in the light of the passion of God, pastoral ministry must be prophetic.

Prophecy and Prophetic Ministry

If pastoral ministry must be prophetic, the converse is also true: *In the light of the passion of God, prophetic ministry must be pastoral.* To put it first negatively, a prophetic Christian ministry is always something different from the politicization of the gospel, and the cross of Christ is what makes the difference. Prophetic ministry is, of course, always risky, and the risk should not be avoided for the sake of never offending anyone. But precisely as we engage in the risky business of a public and political expression of the gospel, we must never lose sight of that other dimension of the passion of God that I have called pastoral. God is not only passionate for justice, but also suffers for the redemption of all in Jesus Christ.

The realization of greater freedom and justice will not eliminate all forms of suffering. Cancer, divorce, automobile accidents, and other personal tragedies cannot be ignored or brushed aside as irrelevant to the real social evils that must be attacked. The passion of God not only motivates us to eliminate whatever suffering can be eliminated; it also empowers us to accompany our brothers and sisters into regions of darkness where suffering can no longer be eliminated; it enables and invites us to share suffering when efforts to overcome it prove futile; it frees us to continue a ministry of compassion and shared grief at the point where those who are guided by criteria of utility and success cease their efforts.

Prophetic ministry cannot afford to overlook the importance of personal faith and spiritual discipline. Christian spirituality is training in embracing anguish, darkness, and death that there may be real, rather than artificial, joy, hope, and new life. Consequently, Christian social action is imperiled not only by the attitude of the rich young man who remained captive to a conventional religious righteousness and failed to obey Jesus' radical command to him to sell all and give to the poor (Mark 10:17–31). It is also endangered by the attitude of the disciple who, captive to an unconventional political righteousness, complained that the perfume with which the woman anointed Jesus in anticipation of his death and burial might have been sold and the money given to the poor (Mark 14:3–9). In the first case, we have an example of excessive spiritualization; in the second case, we have an example of politicization. In both cases, we have an avoidance of the reality of suffering and death on the way to new life.[9]

The church and theology today may profitably ask the question, What can the 1980s learn from the 1960s? Speaking autobiographically, Dennis McCann answers that it is not enough simply to goad people into action. There must be a vital faith, a new vision, and a spiritual discipline that sustain and guide their commitment. If Christ's presence is elusive in proclamation and prayer, it is no less ambiguous in movements of liberation. This is simply to say that we need to cultivate a faith and theology "that will allow us to live with the ultimate ambiguity of Christian social action even as we continue to be involved."[10] McCann's point is close to my own: that prophetic ministry must also be pastoral; that we must retrieve not only the meaning of the passion of God as God's partisanship for the poor, but also the meaning of the passion of God as the mystery of God's suffering with and for the whole groaning creation. When we freely share the suffering of others, we participate in the suffering love of God, whose ultimate triumph is promised in the resurrection of the crucified Christ.

Pastoral sensitivity shapes prophetic ministry in several ways. It requires, in the first place, a continuous distinction of faith from ideology. In faith, we open ourselves radically to the mercy of God, entrust ourselves to God, and seek to love God with all our heart, soul, mind, and strength. As believers, we are not committed first of all to a cause or to a program, but to God made known in the crucified and risen Jesus Christ. In faith, we may make use of various world views, ideologies, and social criticisms. But faith is never exhausted by any of these. Faith that is oriented to the passion of God refuses to become a premature theology of glory. Although Christians hope for the completed reign of Christ in all the earth, they respect the difference between this reign and any society, institution, or movement in the present. Always precarious, the life of faith requires a cruciform and disciplined spirituality that sustains and strengthens Christian involvement in the social and political spheres, while preventing the merger of faith into some currently popular ideology.

Second, if God is the suffering God whose power is expressed decisively in the passion story of the gospel, then the way of sacrificial love must never give in to a spirit of vengeance and indiscriminate force. It is not enough to attack the misuse of power. Rather, a new form of power must find real expression in Christian community and the life of discipleship. All our understandings of power, divine and human, must be continually examined, criticized, and transformed in the light of the gospel. The question of the nature of the power of God and the question of the proper exercise of human power are interlocked. The power of God made known decisively in Jesus Christ, the crucified and living Lord, is neither sheer almightiness nor mere impotence. It is the self-limiting and other-affirming power of agapic love that makes for freedom, justice, and lasting community. Only as we undergo a conversion in our understanding of what is truly powerful are we able to withstand the temptation to confuse the power of the gospel with the coercive and dominative power that we seek to overcome in our struggles against injustice and oppression.[11]

Finally, because the God who freely suffers for us is the God who raises the dead, brings something out of nothing, and creates a new heaven and a new earth, we are em-

132

powered to live in hope in the face of defeat, disappointment, and, ultimately, death. Marxist revolutionaries have no answer to the question that death poses for all human endeavors. Why continue to struggle against evil if everything finally collapses into nothingness? Why hope and work for a new, more just order of society if so many die before its achievement and only those who are alive at the time of that far-off future event will enjoy it? Christian hope is a staggeringly bold and inclusive hope. It refuses to abandon the dead to hopelessness. It refuses to give up hope for the body and for the whole cosmic order. The Christian hope, rooted in the passion and resurrection of Christ, includes the living, the not-yet-born, and the dead.

Thus, by distinguishing faith from ideology, love from dominative power, and hope from all utopianism, the importance of the pastoral dimension of a prophetic ministry becomes clear.

Summary

I have contended that the human situation today is aptly described by the word apathy. I have also argued that some of our familiar images of God serve only to confirm the apathy and desensitization of people. This is the cultural and religious situation in which contemporary theologies are discovering new depths of meaning in the symbol of the passion of God. It is bold and iconoclastic to speak to a human situation characterized by numbness and banality. It aims to shatter the idols of authoritarian power and to call us to partnership with the God whose power is sovereign, suffering, liberating love. I have tried to show that the two most prominent interpretations of this symbol—God's passionate advocacy of justice for the poor and God's own suffering with and for all who are afflicted—are not mutually exclusive, but require each other for mutual enrichment and correction. These two interpretations of the passion of God are related to each other like law and gospel. The law without the gospel is a killing command; the gospel without the law is cheap and sentimental grace. Only gospel *and* law, only God's reconciling passion *and* God's partisanship for the poor, only our participation in both dimensions of the passion of God can make possible our movement from the bondage of apathy to liberative Christian ministry.

CHAPTER 7

Latin-American Liberation Theology: Pastoral Action as the Basis for the Prophetic Task

Jorge Lara-Braud

I ONCE HEARD GUSTAVO GUTIÉRREZ, THE LEADING EXPO-
nent of Latin-American liberation theology, tell a story. He
made an unannounced visit to his alma matter in Belgium, the
University of Louvain. A doctoral student about to embark on
a dissertation on Latin-American liberation theology heard
about it and began eagerly to look for him. After passing him
by more than once—Gutiérrez is notoriously casual in ap-
parel, short of stature, and proletarian in appearance—the
student finally found him with the help of a university professor. Not quite convinced, he asked the Peruvian theologian,
"You are Gustavo Gutiérrez, the father of liberation theology?" Gutiérrez responded, "Well, since we celibates never
get to father anything, this time I'll be vain and will confess to
the paternity charge." Both laughed heartily, shook hands,

Jorge Lara-Braud, Ph.D., is professor of theology and culture at San
Francisco Theological Seminary, San Francisco, California.

and sat on the grass. The instant friendship emboldened the student to come to the point. "What do you liberation theologians *really* believe?"

"Well, let me see, what *do* we believe?" (I can imagine that impish look that comes over him when he is about to say something both commonsensical and profound.) "Ah, yes, we believe in . . . God . . . the father . . . almighty, maker-of-heaven-and-earth . . . and what else? Oh, yes, we believe in Jesus Christ, his only Son, our Lord, who was conceived by the Holy Ghost . . ." (he raced through the rest of the creed, like a breathless child afraid to stop lest the portion of the catechism just memorized be forgotten). He did slow down to end his collective confession on a note of sobriety and joy: ". . . the forgiveness of sins, the resurrection of the body, and the life everlasting." And, for good measure, he added a solemn "Amen."

Exasperated, the student exclaimed, "I don't get it; what, then, is the point?"

This time Gutiérrez turned utterly serious: "The point is whether the creed can be the faith of the poor." That led, I am sure, to a mini-exposition on liberation theology which the student was not likely to forget. My regret is that I did not hear the exposition, and that I instead have to search for something of the same significance in the larger work of Gutiérrez and his colleagues.

I like the story not only because it is vintage Gutiérrez,[1] but also because it points to the poor as the link between the pastoral and the prophetic in Latin-American liberation theology. I like the story also because it suggests how radically orthodox is the doctrinal content of this much misunderstood theology.

Today's Latin-American Church Setting: A Massive Religious Reformation

More important than liberation theology itself is the revival of church life from which it springs. We are witnessing in

Latin America, since the 1960s, a religious reformation possibly of greater scale than the Protestant Reformation of the sixteenth century. This time it takes place in the mainstream of Roman Catholic church life, with considerable fallout effect on the more ecumenical Protestant communities.

The parallels between the two reformations are striking. The Bible is being read by the masses. Jesus Christ is found again as companion and friend of the marginals. Communities of the faithful, largely under lay leadership, gather around the word and sacraments, as they deal with their agonies and their hopes. The priesthood of all believers is reestablished as the foundation of all the church's ministry. Tyranny is challenged in the name of the God of exodus, in the idiom of the eighth-century prophets, and in unison with the Magnificat. The realm of God is announced as Christ's sure promise of a just society. In his crucifixion, Jesus takes up the crucifixion of every faithful follower, and in his resurrection, the victory of every martyrdom. And to proclaim these truths, God raises gifted leaders who are both pastors and prophets.

But there are major differences in the two reformations. The one before grew out of the question whether one could be saved by works or by grace. This one hinges on whether the life-giving justice of God can save the masses of the poor from the death-dealing injustice of the rich. The previous reformation gave rise to bloody religious wars that were fought with relatively balanced military power. This one has triggered a war against the poor in which they put their numbers, their commitments, and their faith against the military technology, the political repression, and the economic might of indigenous elites aided by powerful international allies. The reformation of the sixteenth century in Europe came, in the end, to benefit primarily the new bourgeoise. The reformation of the twentieth century in Latin America is meant primarily to redeem the poor from every oppression that offends God and enslaves people. At stake is what Gutiérrez told the student at Louvain: "Whether the creed can be the faith of the poor."

An Improbable History Behind This Reformation and the Emergence of Liberation Theology[2]

The starting point of Latin-American liberation theology is the sphere of historical facts, particularly those having to do with the engagement of the Christian community in building a society more in keeping with the love of God for all. By tracing the historical facts that led to the emergence of this theology, we may approximate its own methodological perspective.

I cannot, of course, in the compass of a brief overview attempt more than a thumbnail sketch of religious and societal developments.[3] As is well known, the Roman Catholicism of Latin America, coming from Spain and Portugal, represented a rigid response to the challenge of the Protestant Reformation. In other European countries, Catholicism was much more influenced by Protestantism, so that a certain religious pluralism was eventually to emerge. For Latin America, that confrontation would have to wait until the latter half of the nineteenth century, becoming more intense and capable of interpenetration in the years immediately preceding and following Vatican Council II (1962–65). Beginning in the 1850s, Latin-American Protestant missions sowed the seeds for an "evangelical" community that would not reach accelerated growth until the decades of the 1940s and 1950s.

From the conquest of Latin America begun by Columbus in 1492 to the beginning of the wars of independence in 1808, Roman Catholicism served as a powerful instrument of colonization for Spain and Portugal. The triumvirate of power had been firmly established: the military, the landed aristocracy, and the Catholic Church. With few exceptions, missionaries gave their blessing to a pervasive system of oppression over indigenous populations, African slaves, and mestizos (offspring of Iberians and Indians). Political independence left the triumvirate practically intact until the Mexican revolution of 1910–17. By then, the colonial powers were no longer Spain or Portugal, but England and the United States, with the latter predominant in military and economic power. There was consistency in this outcome. The Monroe Doctrine of 1823 had pointedly claimed Latin America for the United States as its sphere of influence and therefore off limits to European nations. Colonialism had yielded to neocolonialism, and its effects on the vast majority were no less oppressive. The landed aristocracies became the entrepreneurial allies of heavy U.S. investment, for which the military, now trained and equipped largely by the United States, became the guarantor through a policy later to be known as "national security."

The Church began to sense the peril of its failure to reform in the face of large numbers of conversions to Protestantism. But after three and a half centuries of suppressing innovation in thought and action, it had neither ideological insight nor institutional flexibility to claim the loyalty of those whom it counted as its own through baptism. Besides, by mid-twentieth century, it faced a massive legacy of anticlericalism and nonparticipation in its sacramental life. But Protestantism was not necessarily the option for the inactive or the disaffected. A Catholic in Latin America may condemn the Church as an institution, but one seldom ceases to consider oneself *católica* or *católico*.

Protestantism was actually welcomed by the progressive sectors and liberal governments. It appeared as the carrier of the kind of modernizing force that had made the United States and western Europe democratic and industrialized nations. Except, however, for the Pentecostals, whose emergence was to be felt in the period preceding and following World War II, the other Protestants succeeded in attracting upper-lowers and lower-middles who in turn became a thriving, well-disciplined, and politically conservative bourgeoisie of limited numbers.[4]

Conversion to Protestantism, whether in the 1850s or the 1950s, meant the adoption of the piety and culture of the rural Bible Belt, or small-town America, of the nineteenth century, with all its pietism, individualism, and anti-Romanism, rendered more acute by the native hostility put up by the Roman Catholic Church. Even the Pentecostals, where they thrived, as they did most dramatically among the Chilean poor, limited their political involvement to securing guarantees for a separatist religious-cultural existence of their own.[5]

As earlier in Europe, Latin America, by the 1950's, had clearly seen the end of the old Christendom, which is to say that society was no longer under religious tutelage. Could a *new* Christendom be possible? The Roman Catholic Church felt that it could. Following certain pastoral experiments in Europe, it sought a policy of "two places." One would be the renewal of the Church from within by a renewed Christianization of the laity. The other would be the re-Christianization of society through youth, labor, and political organizations embodying the social teachings of the Church and led by its laypeople. The chief theoretician was neo-Thomist philosopher Jacques Maritain.[6]

For a time, the policy seemed to succeed. To this day, one of its accomplishments is the continuing existence of "Christian Democratic" parties, the best known being the one led by President Eduardo Frei in Chile just before the Allende government. The success was short-lived. It was not long before these lay groups, sensing the need for more than reform in the economy and in politics, took positions considerably beyond that which the Church could tolerate. Indeed, if their radical options had won, the Church's alliance with the oligarchies would have ended and its social weight would have collapsed. By the early 1960s, instead, the lay groups were disbanded, but not before some of the leaders shifted over to

140

unions and parties of the radical left, where these were still tolerated.[7]

The victory of the Cuban revolution in 1959 dramatized more than any other event the political and economic crisis of the inter-American system. In its wake came the first Development Decade, whose chief expression was John F. Kennedy's Alliance for Progress, and which, paradoxically, or perhaps logically, was followed by the militarization of most Latin-American regimes. Development demanded stability, particularly the massive infusion of American and local investment. Modernization and industrialization ended up requiring the leadership of generals and the growing erosion of what democratic freedoms existed in the name of averting "another Cuba."

The notion of development retained, however, some of its seductive allure for a few years. This was true until a new cadre of sophisticated Latin-American social scientists adopted the viewpoint no longer of highly advanced countries of the "center," but of nations on the "periphery," and began to elaborate a *theory of dependence*. In essence, they documented the fact that underdevelopment at the periphery was the inevitable counterpart of development at the center. Further, with the aid of theoretical contributions from Marx, they affirmed the need, in words of Gustavo Gutiérrez:

> to assure the change from the capitalistic mode of production to the socialist mode, that is to say, to one oriented towards a society in which man can begin to live freely and humanly. . . . The goal is not only better living conditions, a radical change of structures, a social revolution; it is more: the continuous creation, never ending, of a new way to be a man, a *permanent cultural* revolution.[8]

The papal encyclicals of the 1960s—*Mater et Magistra* and *Pacem in Terris* of John XXIII, and *Populorum Progressio* of Paul VI—gave considerable attention to development, the latter discussing it as its central theme. However, it now appended the adjective integral to it. This meant that the

Church's social teaching advocated the total transformation of the person and the structures that affect his or her life. Significantly, liberal capitalism came in for a scathing condemnation by Paul VI. Referring to it as a "baseless theory," he condemned it for considering profit "the key motive for economic progress, competition as the supreme law of economics, and private ownership of the means of production as an absolute right that has no limits and carries no corresponding obligations [*Populorum Progressio*, I, No. 26, 1967]."

The more realistic theory of dependence began to be elaborated in Vatican II's Constitution on the Church and the Modern World (*Gaudium et Spes*).[9] However, it also criticized the concept of "total emancipation of humanity wrought solely by human effort" and a human liberation reduced to purely economic and social dimensions.[10]

This brings us to the threshold of the historic Medellín Conference of August 1968 of CELAM II (The Second Conference of Latin-American Bishops). Opened by Paul VI, it was seen as the occasion for Vatican II to be interpreted in the light of Latin-American realities. A Peruvian theologian, Gustavo Gutiérrez, was to emerge as its most influential contributor. He was then forty years old, having served as pastor and teacher for eight years in Lima after extensive graduate studies at the Universities of Louvain and Lyon and at the Gregorian in Rome. Medellín's sections on Peace and on Justice, the most frequently quoted as theological breakthroughs, bear his clear imprint.[11] But he was by no means alone in giving priority to liberation categories over those of development. The clear historical and harmful failure of developmentalist policies had been repudiated even by a number of bishops who years before had advocated a new Christendom and the social and economic prescriptions emanating from advanced capitalist societies.

The Medellín documents,[12] although by no means a full elaboration of a liberation theology, are nevertheless its authoritative foundation. By this we mean both its initial encouragement as well as its legitimation by Church authorities, at least in its basic perspectives. Such a virtual nihil obstat is what safeguards it from a charge of heterodoxy. The more recent (February 1979) CELAM III, in Puebla, Mexico, rather than disqualifying liberation theology, in a number of important respects confirmed it, although it cannot be claimed that CELAM endorsed liberation theology as such.

Medellín was predominantly a search for pastoral positions for a Church and a continent in revolutionary ferment, which is to say a crisis of such magnitude as to require radical alternatives. It would be too much to claim that it succeeded. To put it another way, it was too much to expect that the weight of traditionalism could quickly yield to a total conversion. However, Medellín did not recoil from calling injustice and oppression in the continent a "sinful situation," because where "social peace does not exist, there we will find social, political, economic and cultural inequalities, there we will find the rejection of the peace of the Lord, and a rejection of the Lord Himself."[13] Nor did it shy away from locating the pervasive presence of violence in the very institutions of society by characterizing their behavior as "institutional violence," which in turn explains the "temptation of violence" to combat it.[14]

When *development* or even *integral development* remains the dominant motif, the assumption is one of catching up, without precision as to what holds back the "underdeveloped." When *liberation* predominates, then its polar opposite, *oppression*, can be identified not only with a new clarity, but the way is then also open for possible redress. Moreover, and more important, the terms now fall squarely within a biblical perspective in which a liberating God in concrete historical acts redeems and emancipates, beginning with the most oppressed: the poor.

It is no coincidence that the issue of the poor was central to

143

Medellín. How can the Church speak the good news of justice and peace to its own impoverished masses? Its answer, admittedly a beginning, is expressed thus:

> The Latin American bishops cannot remain indifferent in the face of the tremendous social injustices existent in Latin America, which keep the majority of our peoples in dismal poverty, which in many cases becomes inhuman wretchedness. A deafening cry pours from the throats of millions, asking their pastors for a liberation that reaches them from nowhere else. . . . Christ our Savior not only loved the poor, but rather "being rich He became poor," and lived in poverty. His mission centered on advising the poor of their liberation and He founded His Church as the sign of that poverty among men.[15]

Significant also is the rubric "Poverty of the Church," under which Medellín dealt with the poor. In penitential terms, the trappings of pomp and circumstance are renounced where those still exist, so that solidarity with the poor means that "we make ours their problems and their struggles. . . . This has to be concretized in criticism of injustice and oppression."[16]

Although opening up germinal analyses and directions, Medellín is actually not as radical as it might appear. It does not entirely abandon development categories. It is a transition between advanced but still moderate social teachings and a preferential option for the poor, with far-reaching implications yet to be worked out. It does affirm the demand for transformed structures but only in the context of transformed new persons, "who know how to be truly free and responsible according to the light of the Gospel."[17] It does not confuse temporal progress and the kingdom of Christ; nevertheless, quoting Vatican II, such progress "to the extent that it can contribute to the better ordering of human society, is of vital importance to the kingdom of Christ."[18]

On these grounds, it disqualifies both "liberal capitalism" and the "Marxist system":

Both militate against the dignity of the human person. One takes for granted the primacy of capital, its power and its discriminatory utilization in the function of profit making. The other, although it ideologically supports a kind of humanism, is more concerned with collective man, and in practice becomes a totalitarian concentration of state power. We must denounce the fact that Latin America sees itself caught between these two options and remains dependent on one or other of the centers of power which control its economy.[19]

This passage illustrates better perhaps than any other Medellín's leaving open alternatives that, when worked out, were seriously to polarize the Catholic Church. If *liberal* capitalism and the Marxist *system* are rejected, more than one substitute may be inferred. One of these will be the socialistic option characteristic of liberation theology. Its exponents will argue that capitalism, whether liberal (laissez-faire), monopolistic, or oligopolistic (the transnational corporations), leaves no structural possibility to poor countries but their further impoverishment. Their economies are inevitably captive to the exigencies of the alliance between local oligarchies and the capitalist centers abroad, the behavior of both being determined by the maximization of profit. How else, they ask, can one explain that even when, statistically, per capita income keeps increasing, there are proportionately many more poor than before the first Development Decade (1960s) and before the Second (1970s)? Could this be the root cause of what Medellín identifies as "that misery, a collective fact, expressed as injustice which cries to the heavens"?[20]

But Medellín clearly rejected the Marxist system. Isn't the espousal of socialism, then, contradictory? The answer of most liberation theologians is that socialism and the Marxist *system* are not necessarily synonymous. In fact, some harshly criticize the systems, for example, of the People's Republic of China, the Union of Soviet Socialist Republics, and, to a lesser degree, that of Cuba.[21] Actually, their argument continues, "third ways" (between capitalism and socialism) invari-

145

ably are absorbed by capitalism, thereby causing the expansion of misery, as, for example, during the Christian Democracy of Eduardo Frei in Chile (with its "revolution in peace" posture) or the Peruvian military "revolution" of 1968 (a failed populist challenge to multinational capitalism).[22]

Later I shall touch on the thorny issue of the use of Marxism in both theology and political action. What I have sought to do is to suggest how the Medellín conference has been appealed to by growing numbers not only as the theological legitimation for recasting Christian faith around the liberation-oppression axis, but also as the stimulus for a pastoral stance that takes the side of the poor.

At this juncture it is appropriate to focus attention on a parallel development among Latin-American Protestants. In fact, the case could be made that the first stage of liberation theology is to be found in a Protestant vanguard of the early and mid-sixties gathered in a continental movement known as ISAL (Church and Society in Latin America).[23] Born in a conference in Huampaní, Peru, in 1961, it set out to read the scriptures, reflect theologically, and search for new forms of Christian witness in the light of a continent undergoing profound transformations. In the early years, the chief theoretician was Richard Shaull, for two decades an American Presbyterian missionary in Colombia and Brazil and more recently professor of ecumenics at Princeton Theological Seminary. In its seminal years (1961–65), ISAL oscillated between a developmentalist approach and a revolutionary perspective. The latter position was strongly represented by ISAL theologians at the 1966 World Council of Churches Conference on Church and Society.[24] The "theology of revolution" began, as of that time, to be identified with them. This somewhat inexact identification did not last long. A few years later, no less inexactly, it passed on to European theologians, chiefly Johannes B. Metz and Jürgen Moltmann. The former was to emerge as the chief proponent of "political theology,"[25] and the latter, the chief proponent of the "theology of hope."[26]

By 1966, ISAL was focusing on the theory of dependence, anticipating much of the reflection of their later Roman Catholic counterparts. The 1966 El Tabo (Chile) conference[27] makes a shift from a neoorthodox position (largely Barthian) to "a theology of God's transforming action in history," as José Míguez Bonino rightly observes, "greatly indebted to Paul Lehmann and Richard Shaull until Rubem Alves gave it a creative expression in critical dialogue with Marcuse on the one hand and Moltmann on the other."[28]

In contrast with Roman Catholic liberation theologians, whose emergence and influence are to be located in the mainstream of Church life, the ISAL group was never able to establish a parallel relationship to Protestant communities. Although solidly basing its theological work on the very same Bible that those communities so highly prized, ISAL's positions, where known, were generally seen by fellow Protestants as a betrayal of Christian faith to secularization, politics, and even to socialism, which then, as now, was generally equated with communism. A widely read book by U.S. evangelical missionary Peter Wagner, published in 1970, illustrates this highly negative assessment of a number of Protestant theologians, almost all related to ISAL.[29] His was and may yet be the prevailing Latin-American Protestant view against a theology that he terms "radical" rather than "evangelical."

His main criticisms of the radicals are:

1. Socioeconomic concerns are given priority over "the mission of the Church—which is to persuade men and women to be reconciled individually to God."[30]

2. "They judge evangelical theology not in terms of how true it is to the Bible or how it will result in the salvation of souls, but what it will do to promote social justice."[31]

3. The commandment to preach the gospel is placed on a parity or is complementary with a commandment to participate in the redemptive work of Christ in the world, which is nowhere to be found in the scriptures.[32]

4. Opting for concrete, "worldly" situations as Christian

choices is not only to disregard their ambiguity, but also to raise "the possibility of failing to make the offer of salvation available to mankind."[33]

5. The forces that oppose the action of God are not taken seriously enough. This is a failure to come to grips with the biblical concept of supernatural, not just natural, forces of evil that "play a sinister and important part."[34]

6. Universalism (God's saving action for all) contradicts the biblical teaching that only those who hear the gospel and believe in Jesus Christ are saved.[35]

Criticisms of this sort, quite valid if the premises are granted, were being made of ISAL before it adopted a clear Marxist analysis of dependence, or before it chose to divide itself into national groups, which enabled it to join hands with Roman Catholic partners and to labor in more localized struggles for social justice. The movement as such ceased to exist in the mid-seventies, partly because of the desire to narrow the gap between it and the churches. Another reason was that in some countries, such as Brazil, Chile, Argentina, Uruguay, and Bolivia, identification with ISAL had become not only a barrier to church fellowship, but, worse yet, an additional vulnerability to imprisonment, torture, and exile at the hands of national security forces. Sadly, that was the fate of not a few of its members.

Oftentimes the credibility, power, and dignity of a movement are measured and fortified by the number and quality of its martyrs. The Christian liberation movement of Latin America is a case in point. Its exemplar is Fr. Camilo Torres, a Colombian priest who was killed as a guerrilla insurgent in the village of El Carmen, Colombia, on February 15, 1966. From an aristocratic family and expected to become a lawyer, he instead chose the priesthood out of a deep commitment to the poor. After completing theological studies with high honors, he was ordained and shortly thereafter pursued graduate studies in sociology at Louvain. Two of his years there overlapped with those of a young theologian, Gustavo Gutiérrez, whose course of studies in philosophy and psychology had preceded his by three years. They became devoted friends.

Returning to Colombia as teacher and chaplain at the National University, Camilo, as he was affectionately known, analyzed in depth the established order and the Church's position of privilege. That led him to question both. His intense dialogue with students and the indigent persuaded him of the need to press the Church's social influence into the denunciation of injustice and the annunciation of a more humane society. At the peak of his popularity, the Cardinal Primate sought to silence him and, not succeeding, removed him from his university post and reduced him to lay status. Camilo never ceased to consider himself a priest. Still a reformer, and trusting the electoral process as the best nonviolent means to bring about a structural change, he called for a coalition of opposition parties in hopes of breaking the monopoly by rotation of the liberal and conservative parties, both representing the oligarchy. It was futile. His next appeal was for massive civil disobedience in imitation of Martin Luther King Jr. The response was massive repression. It was then that he became convinced that only armed revolution was left as a viable alternative. Setting out to join the guerrillas, he wrote:

I have ceased to say mass [in order] to practice love for people in temporal, economic and social spheres. When the people have nothing against me, when they have carried the revolution, then I will return to offering mass, God willing. I think that in this way I follow Christ's injunction, " . . . leave your gift on the altar and go first to be reconciled to your brothers [and sisters]."[36]

Six months later, he was killed in an ambush. Even for the many who questioned his fatal decision, his example, more than any protest or pronouncement, recalled the dangerous memory of an ancient truth: "The blood of the martyrs is the seed of the church." Others, many others, were to follow, and for each of the fallen, hundreds were to rise. As Gustavo

Gutiérrez has written, "Seldom have we lived through a period of greater ferment, liveliness or creativity of experiences and insights, because we had seldom confronted more decisively the propagators of fear, death and sterile caution."[37]

The quotation is taken from an introduction to a collection of testimonials out of the Latin-American Church's struggle during the years from 1973 to 1978. It follows two previous, similar collections, one of them translated into English.[38] The three taken together constitute a multitude of witnesses of how prophetic, courageous, and massive is the liberation posture of bishops, regional and national episcopates, clergy groups, religious orders, and Christian lay groups. It is on this massive record, still growing, that liberation theology stands.

Solidarity, Pastoral Conversion, and a New Way of Doing Theology

Given the realities of "institutionalized violence" and a "situation of sin" documented by this history, and especially by Medellín, the bishops of Latin America agreed with their theologians that the Church's chief pastoral priority was to take the side of the poor. Shortly after Medellín, the clearest language found to express this pastoral position was the now-famous phrase "the preferential option for the poor." When the Latin-American bishops met again in Puebla, in 1979, adherence to this precise language became the test of pastoral fidelity. Although a monumental effort was made by conservatives in the continent and by some in the Vatican curia for striking "a more moderate position," Puebla not only affirmed Medellín, but also stated in unequivocal terms: "We affirm the need for conversion on the part of the whole church to a preferential option for the poor, an option aimed at their integral liberation."[39]

The language of conversion is instructive. The bishops are giving testimony to a number of claims made by liberation

150

theology with respect to the nature of theology and the pastoral task in which the predominant issues are oppression and liberation.

According to Latin-American theologians, theology itself is an act of solidarity, based in turn in an experience of conversion to the poor. Until now, according to them, the dominant theology of Europe and the United States has assumed a kind of elegant disengagement from daily pastoral tasks.[40] It seems possible, for instance, to produce impressive tomes on the ways of God without the slightest experiential verification among God's people. It is perplexing indeed that theology should be done in circumstances, such as often prevail in Europe, where church life has virtually collapsed. Theology done apart from dialogue with the faithful may bear the name theology, but it is not a witness to the biblical God who becomes incarnate in the life of people. That kind of theology, although occasionally mentioning God's special regard for the weak, actually prides itself in being nonpartisan, alleging notions of scientific rigor and fidelity to the reconciling function of God-talk. And yet, such theology is not neutral. Its so-called impartiality is actually a vote for things as they are.

Liberation theologians sustain their case with a barrage of pastoral arguments: the God of the Bible—the subject of theology—is clearly biased for the poor, the widow, the orphan, the abused. The same God witnesses to the divine self in verifiable historical acts; those who witness to God as theologians should not be more spiritual than God. Because the self-disclosure of God is in action, specifically *just* action, theology that does not flow from participation in such action is at best pretheological and at worst propagandist.

If, instead, theology is an act of solidarity with the poor, other things have to precede it. The Church itself must undergo the kind of conversion espoused by Medellín and Puebla, the way for which was prepared by the aggiornamento of Vatican II.

Conversion begins when the Bible is returned to the

151

masses for their own interpretation under the guidance of the Spirit. The church need not fear their originality. Properly shepherded, they will enrich the church's faith. A true pastor is one who teaches well by learning from believers out of a common engagement with the Word of God amid the tragedies and joys of the community's daily life. A lucid example is Ernesto Cardenal's experience with a congregation of peasants and fisherfolk in Solentiname, Nicaragua. Four volumes of that kind of shared Bible exposition now enrich, in Spanish and in English, the pastoral wisdom of the church under the title *The Gospel in Solentiname.*[41]

Conversion continues by understanding the God incarnate in Jesus, following Jesus in the vicissitudes of his contemporary surrogates: the hungry, the thirsty, the naked, the sick, the stranger, the prisoner. One of the ablest modern works on Christology is the book by Jesuit Jon Sobrino of El Salvador, *Christology at the Crossroads.*[42] Significantly, the Spanish subtitle is "Esbozo a partir del seguimiento del Jesús histórico" (An Approach from the Following of the Historical Jesus). His thesis is that a true doctrine of Christ emerges only from a contemporary companionship with Jesus in circumstances parallel to those of his time. Sobrino touches here on a central pastoral conviction of liberation theologians. The poor, among whom one follows Jesus, enjoy a "hermeneutical privilege," that is, their very location in the world grants them a direct access of interpretation to the biblical revelation, for the Bible was written chiefly by and for people like them. Moreover, they are privileged objects of God's biased love, and in them, Jesus Christ is present as nowhere else.

Conversion implies sharing in the hopes and struggles of the poor as God uses them to restore the intended creation. The very ability of the pastor to trust the future and to contribute to such a future hinges on his or her capacity to hope against hope, as the struggling Christian poor do.

A theologian-pastor converted to the poor will soon discover that poverty is not accidental, but the result of unjust economic arrangements. Here is the point at which liberation theologians, trying to discern the will of God, have been driven to the resources of the social sciences and, inevitably, to a selective use of Marxist tools of analysis, particularly in the area of ideological and economic mechanisms of oppression. Nothing about Latin-American liberation theology is more misunderstood than its use of Marxist analysis, despite the repeated reminders by its spokespersons that what is in question are tools of analysis and not the Marxist system, that to attempt to understand modern economic theory without Marx is tantamount to using psychotherapy without reference to Freud or Jung, and that theology in previous epochs has relied heavily on the philosophical works of pagans like Plato and Aristotle without thereby de-Christianizing Christian theology.

Of course, what does not escape liberation theologians is the degree to which the ideology of capitalism has become the practical faith of the consumer society, so that *any* use of capitalism's chief critic is perceived not as a critique of an economic system, but as an attack on the religion that that system has become.

No one has written on Marx's contribution to theology more lucidly or courageously among Latin-American liberation theologians than U.S.-trained Argentinian Methodist José Míguez Bonino. In his book *Christians and Marxists*,[43] Míguez has identified the four basic insights of Marxism for anyone who is seriously concerned to be a Christian ally of the poor:

1. The understanding of history as inevitably dependent on the human process through which goods are produced to satisfy human need

2. The recognition that the human being is not a single individual, but a communal unity in the form of a concrete social formation

3. The fact of class struggle arising from an economic sys-

tem whose very logic creates an antagonism of classes, so that the emancipation of the oppressed implies the creation of a new society

4. The notion of praxis, that is, that true knowledge results from concrete human action, that theory has meaning only as it leads to a course of action that proves significant, and that action itself becomes the test of theory

If Míguez is correct, these four contributions could hardly subvert Christian faith. The disturbing truth is that their parallels are to be found in some form in every prophetic utterance of the Bible having to do with the clash between justice and injustice.

Robert McAfee Brown, whose grasp of Latin-American liberation theology is more thorough and sympathetic than that of any other American or European scholar, makes this point when he calls attention to five illustrative passages that bear out the claim that to know God is to do justice within the realities of modes of production, social formations, the struggle for equality, and the verification of truth in action. In so doing, he echoes Míguez Bonino's four basic insights derived from Marx. Those passages are:

1. The God Who Takes Sides (Exodus 1:8–14; 2:23–25; 3:7–10ff.)
2. To Know God Is to Do Justice (Jeremiah 22:13–16; 31:31–34)
3. The True Worship (Isaiah 58:6–7)
4. Liberty to the Oppressed (Luke 4:16–30)
5. The Judgment of the Nations (Matthew 25:31–46)

Not surprisingly, he concludes his exegesis of these passages by saying that "we American Christians, in our ideological captivity are likely to have missed [these emphases]" and that may explain why "we seem to have been reading a different book from our Third World friends."[44] The strange kindredness between scripture and capitalism's most celebrated foe has been brilliantly documented by Mexican theologian

José Porfirio Miranda in a number of books, the best known of which is *Marx and the Bible*. Significantly, he has also, just as brilliantly, documented the distortion of Marx by Marxists.[45]

Justice and Liberation Are the Issue

The issue, however, for the new Christian communities of Latin America is not Marx. The issue is the dawning vision of a just society, largely inspired by biblical sources amid a recrudescence of oppression. The pastoral task is, therefore, a prophetic defense of the right of the poor majorities to translate their vision into the creation of a just social order. This raises the question of what is meant by justice. Liberation theologians have a great deal to say about it. For the meaning and content of justice in this section, I am indebted to Ismael Garcia's recent unpublished doctoral dissertation written for the faculty of the Divinity School of the University of Chicago under the title "The Concept of Justice in Latin American Theology of Liberation" (1983). (The discussion of liberation is adapted from my 1980 monograph *What Is Liberation Theology?*.)

First of all, justice is a contextual reality. As José Míguez Bonino has pointed out,

> it is important to point out from the beginning that there are no abstract ethics in Scripture. Love, justice or freedom are never extolled or required as general values or ideal norms, but always embodied in concrete relationships: it is justice to the poor, the orphan, the widow, the foreigner; it is love for a specific neighbor or a specific enemy, freedom from a particular slavery: political or economic, or from the curse of the law, or from the captivity of death.[46]

This contrasts with the bourgeois concept that roots justice in individualism, universality, and equality as ideal norms. Important and humane and even biblical-sounding as such norms are, they have served to legitimize social arrangements

155

of pronounced oppression, as in Latin America. It makes, therefore, a great deal of difference where one ultimately locates the meaning of justice. For Latin-American liberation theologians, that is found in the Bible and, more specifically, in the prophetic tradition that culminates with the ministry of Jesus. This is how Miranda states the case:

> The only God who in the past had shown that his sole concern was justice for the oppressed was Yahweh. He was the only one whose revelatory intervention in human history had consisted in an immense act of justice. At the moment when someone . . . does justice to the poor and the despised, this is the God who inspires and guides him. . . . In order for Yahweh to be revealed effectively in Jesus Christ, the efficacy of the works must be of the same efficacy of the word, namely, the unmistakable revelation of the God who does not let himself be neutralized, because he is God only in the imperative of justice.[47]

Ismael Garcia, after reviewing much of the work of Miranda, Gutiérrez, Míguez Bonino, and Hugo Assmann, rightly concludes that for Latin-American liberation theology, "the needs of the poor provide the material content for the formal definition of justice. . . . The satisfaction of the needs of the poor becomes the criterion by which to measure the justice quality of a given state of affairs."[48]

Because we are concerned here with the relationship between the pastoral and the prophetic, we must search in liberation theology for concrete ways in which justice, as a biblical and theological category, becomes contextually specific. The best clue for this search has been given in the work of Gutiérrez dealing with the concept of liberation. In a much-quoted passage, he introduces us to the richness of it and, in the process, illumines the virtual synonymity between liberation and salvation as it is found in his work and in the work of his theological colleagues. This is how he states it:

> Liberation . . . is a complex, differentiated unity, which has

within itself various levels of meaning which are not to be confused: economic, social and political liberation; liberation which leads to the creation of a new human in a new society of solidarity; and liberation from sin and entrance into communion with God and with all humans. The first corresponds to the level of scientific rationality, which supports real and effective political action; the second stands at the level of utopia, of historical projections, . . . the third is on the level of faith.[49]

The first level or approach of liberation points to the insights gained when, as we have seen earlier, the frame of reference is no longer *development-underdevelopment,* but *liberation-oppression.* This points to economic, social, and political achievements.

The second level of liberation is the creation of a new society. It sees both the human person and history in a perspective considerably more hopeful than what we find in much European and American Protestantism. This is not Bonhoeffer's "a world come of age." Rather, what is involved here is that Christian theological stream that, although taking sin quite seriously, especially in its structural forms, nevertheless views men and women as being capable of creating a new person and a qualitatively different society, even though many may not be Christian. The horizon, therefore, is one of confidence, of "untested feasibilities" (Freire), rather than the sort of Niebuhrian "Christian realism" that emphasizes the sin-tainted nature of even the loftiest human accomplishment. Precisely this contrast of perspectives led to a famous debate in the pages of *Christianity and Crisis* in 1973, in response to Thomas A. Sanders' characterization of Latin-American liberation theology as "soft utopianism."[50]

The debate about the extent of human capability and human responsibility is an old one. In one form, it appeared in the dispute between Augustine and Pelagius about whether men and women could be saved by grace alone or could cooperate with grace. In the Reformation, the Protestant stress on justification by grace through faith challenged the medieval

157

Catholic view of human action contributing to or earning salvation. The tendency in some Protestant thought to stress justification to the exclusion of sanctification led to a quietism that rejected the possibility of breakthroughs of true justice, although others recognized that sanctification was responsible action in the presence of God's grace. There was the further tendency in extreme Calvinist groups to stress predestination to the extent that human beings were completely passive and all events were the outcome of God's decrees. In this century, the rejection of nineteenth-century liberalism by neoorthodoxy, with its revival of the Augustinian stringency as to the nature and extent of original sin, denied or called into question the possibility of human achievement and any real progress in history.

Roman Catholicism, in contrast to Protestantism, has been considerably confident about the human capacity for good because of its much greater attention to people's response to God's grace than to their fall. It is a tradition that trusts men and women far more than it distrusts them. That may be why liberation theology was born in a Catholic continent, even among Protestants. This theology is obstinate in the face of the human negation of grace; it hopes against hope and refuses to give up the human possibility of response.

It is instructive to see what observations Gutiérrez himself makes and what categories he uses when he deals with the second level of liberation as a historical process of humanization. He focuses on the growing self-understanding of man (he writes in prefeminist days) as a "historical being." This he attributes to the emergence of modern science, the techniques of the transformation of nature and the philosophical contributions of Descartes, Kant, Hegel, Marx, Freud, Marcuse, and Teilhard de Chardin. What emerges is a "dynamic and historical conception of man, oriented definitely and creatively towards his future," and a man actually "taking hold of the reins of evolution." For him, "the achievements of humanity are cumulative" within a history moving toward a new way of being human, a global solidarity that liberates people from the exterior pressures of social class, country, or society and from the interior oppressions of alienation and one-dimensionality. In summary, "the goal is not only better conditions, radical change of structures, a social revolution; it is much more: the continuous creation, never ending, of being human, a permanent cultural revolution."[51]

We are at this point in the realm of a rehabilitated notion of utopia. For Latin-American theologians, justice, eschatology, and politics are brought together by the utopian exercise of imagination. To elaborate on what they mean by utopian, I include helpful passages from American theologians Letty Russell and James Cone.

Paulo Freire's classic *The Pedagogy of the Oppressed* (New York: Herder and Herder, 1970) underlines much of Latin-American liberation theology's insights on the verification of truth in action and the way to discern the future. For him, utopia presents itself as denunciation and annunciation. The contradictions of the present are denounced on the basis of a *feasible* new order. The untested feasibilities of justice are announced as the shape of a possible future.

Letty Russell, a Presbyterian feminist theologian, works out a similar perspective dwelling on Paul's notion of *hos me* ("as if not" [1 Corinthians 7:29–30]). Women "are to live *as if not;* as if the facts of the situation are only provisional because of the horizon of freedom. The prolepsis or anticipation of the new world is breaking in and all other aspects cannot be taken with utter seriousness. The gift of God's liberation in Jesus Christ is the only serious matter."[52] She also finds in the categories of *futurum* (the future evolving out of the past) and *adventus* (God's gift of a qualitatively new order) the link between human work and God's grace.

In a similar vein, James Cone writes, "Those who see God's coming liberation breaking into the present must live as if the future is already present in their midst."[53] Conversely, he reminds us, "Usually, when the reality of the political situa-

159

tion dawns upon the oppressed, those who have no vision from another world tend to give up in despair."[54]

This utopian dimension is not necessarily even a religious category. It is a task of imagination, greatly enhanced, of course, by the biblical promises of a new creation (Romans 8) and of a new heaven and a new earth (Revelation 21:1). As such, it is the peculiar contribution of rational but inspired people who here and now live *as if* the blessed alternative is a present reality. As Freire has said, only the oppressed person, the oppressed class can both denounce and announce. Gutiérrez adds, "Only they are capable of working out revolutionary utopias and not conservative or reformist ideologies. The oppressive system's only future is to maintain its present affluence."[55]

For Gutiérrez, there is no immediate relationship between faith and political action. To attempt such a relationship directly leads to a politico-religious messianism with consequences harmful to both faith and politics. The mediation between the two is rather to be found in utopia. It radicalizes the struggle for a new order, a permanent creation. Creation is the encounter between political action and communion with God and other human beings. This communion implies liberation from sin. Faith proclaims the abolition of exploitation: that efforts to bring it about are not in vain, that God assures it, and that "the definitive reality is being built on what is transitory."[56] Only such a view, insists Gutiérrez, "can keep us from any confusion of the kingdom with any historical stage, from any idolatry toward unavoidably ambiguous human achievement, from any absolutizing of revolution."[57]

The third level of liberation is liberation from sin. This is radical liberation because "sin—a breach of friendship with God and others—is according to the Bible the ultimate cause of poverty, injustice and all the oppressions in which men live. . . . Behind an unjust structure there is a personal or collective will responsible—a willfulness to reject God and neighbor." But "a social transformation, no matter how radical it may be, does not automatically achieve the suppression of all evils."[58] *Only* Christ liberates from sin (Galatians 5), and if asked what for, Gutiérrez, following Paul, answers, "To be free to love." The *only* refers to all three levels. They constitute "a single complex process, which finds its deepest sense and its full realization in the saving work of Christ."[59]

Some critics of liberation theology, most recently Schubert M. Ogden, fault it for not distinguishing between redemption and emancipation. Ogden argues that such failure stems from an inadequate doctrine of God, itself the result of a deficient metaphysics. On his premise, liberation theology is not strictly theology, but ethics, which is to say that it is somewhat adequate as to emancipation but definitely inadequate as to redemption.[60] Gutiérrez, as we have just seen above and will continue to observe below, would not recognize himself in such a critique, nor would other liberation theologians, who part company with Marxism when it fails to deal with redemption, that is, overcoming death and living in the joy of resurrection.[61]

At the conclusion of the chapter on "Liberation and Salvation" in his *A Theology of Liberation*, Gutiérrez returns to the three levels of liberation reviewed earlier. He reminds us that "political liberation, the liberation of man throughout history, and liberation from sin and admission to communion with God . . . are all part of a single all-encompassing *salvific* process, but they are to be found at different levels."[62]

Here we enter what for post-Vatican II Roman Catholics may be an entirely appropriate way of viewing the inclusiveness of salvation, but for Protestants presents a difficult if not an unacceptable conception, either because of its "universalism" (the encompassing purpose of God to save the whole world) or its seeming "horizontalism" (the accomplishment of salvation in history, not beyond it). Moreover, at stake in such a view of salvation are matters as serious as coopera-

161

tion with non-Christians, political options between, let us say, socialism and capitalism, styles of evangelization, Christian unity and disunity, pastoral action, and forms of the church.

Curiously, Gutiérrez remarks: "One of the great deficiencies of contemporary theology is the absence of a profound and lucid reflection on the theme of salvation."[63] This sounds strange to a Protestant. If there is one subject on which volumes of Protestant theology have been written, it is salvation. But he was writing in 1970–71, before liberation theology bridged the Catholic-Protestant chasm of Latin America. His point of reference, then, is Roman Catholic theology and especially European. In the compass of three pages he moves from the abandoned position of *extra ecclesia nulla salus* (outside the church no salvation), which he terms "quantitative," to the "qualitative." The latter, he believes, is presupposed although not entirely made explicit in theologically advanced positions of Vatican II. He asserts, therefore, that "man is saved if he opens himself to God and to others, even if he is not clearly aware that he is doing so. This is valid for Christians and non-Christians alike—for all people."[64] At work is the notion of saving grace active in all human beings and all history that never disappeared from the classic Catholic tradition. If taken seriously, this notion destroys the remnant, even in that tradition, of the dualism between natural and supernatural and between a profane and a religious world. "Human existence, in the last instance," he argues, "is nothing but a yes or a no to the Lord," and by way of confirmation, he cites a 1968 pastoral document of CELAM based on Vatican II:

> Men already partly accept communion with God, although they do not explicitly confess Christ as their Lord, insofar as they are moved by grace (*Lumen gentium*, No. 16) sometimes secretly (*Gaudium et Spes*, Nos. 3, 222), renounce their selfishness and seek to create an authentic brotherhood among men. They reject union with God insofar as they turn away

162

from the building up of this world, do not open themselves to others, and culpably withdraw unto themselves. (Mt. 25:31–46).[65]

What is salvation, then? Gutiérrez' deceptively simple answer is "the communion of men with God and the communion of men among themselves . . . something which embraces all human reality, transforms it, and leads it to its fullness in Christ."[66]

The universalist argument of Gutiérrez and of other Roman Catholic liberation theologians is based in part on the sovereignty of God but also on the insight that there is only one human history irreversibly assumed by Christ, so that the history of salvation is its very heart.[67] From a Protestant position, Míguez Bonino states: "It would be more accurate to say that God's sovereignty is realized *polemically* in history. To put it more pointedly, God's sovereignty is an efficacious word that makes history and is itself historicized by summoning and rejecting human beings and people on the basis of God's design."[68] His basis is the conviction that "in the Bible there is no activity that does not have some bearing in human history; and human history is never recounted except in relation to God's sovereignty."[69]

Sin and salvation are, hence, earthly, intrahistorical realities. Inner, personal sin is not disregarded, nor is its need to be forgiven and removed. But the emphasis in liberation theology is less subjective and more social. Sin's eradication requires the removal of conditions that make it more sinful and pervasive. Its form as "personal fracture" derives from what José María González Ruiz calls the "hamartiosphere," the sphere of sin, which, in González' words, quoted by Gutiérrez, is "a kind of parameter or structure which objectively conditions the progress of human history itself."[70] The language, drawn from Teilhard, is reminiscent of the Pauline "principalities and powers," categories dear to Protestant ethicists and activists, with the possible exception that their use is frequently qualified by a Niebuhrian "Christian realism" that assumes they will never be seriously defeated this side of the Second Coming.

Juan Luis Segundo, although sympathetic to European "political theologies" (Metz and Moltmann), faults them as legatees of Luther's position when "they eliminate from theological-political language any term that might suggest a causal relationship between historical activity and the construction of the Kingdom of God."[71] The most they dare, he contends, is the notions of "anticipation" (Moltmann) or "rough draft" (Metz). Hope and faith are released for the future, so when it comes to concrete proposals for the present, they become revolutionary in thought but not in action.[72]

Given the present structures that continue to imprison the poor in their poverty, denying them their right to live in the full-orbed liberation intended by God, nothing less than a radical transformation of society becomes imperative. That is the most demanding link between the pastoral and the prophetic for the new Christian communities of Latin America. To illustrate how that link functions, and to conclude this essay on a note of struggle and hope characteristic of liberation theology, I turn to the Salvadoran model.

To Be Pastoral Is to Be Prophetic: The Salvadoran Model

From what has been said thus far, I hope at least one claim of Latin-American liberation theology is clear: There can be no meaningful God-talk apart from the discernment that comes from God's presence and action among the poor to whom God is definitely partial. It is from that discernment that theology becomes inevitably partisan and inevitably prophetic, because there is much to denounce—but also much to announce.

We sometimes sell the prophets short perhaps by picturing them as being inspired and heroic but not much more than humorless denouncers. The nobility of Latin-American Christian prophets in this massive conversion of the church to the poor is striking not only because of their courage, but also because of their joy and their hope. The model of the biblical prophet has clearly shaped their role. The biblical prophet, although frequently not a pastor, nevertheless speaks the word of God's judgment, always holding out God's invitation to conversion and pointing to a new beginning of love, justice, and peace.[73]

When Latin-American liberation theologians are called on to point specifically to a model of the unity between the pastoral and the prophetic, the inevitable choice is Oscar Arnulfo Romero, the slain archbishop of San Salvador.[74] Of course, I agree heartily, because I came to be one of his close personal friends. Gustavo Gutiérrez' latest book, *We Drink from Our Own Wells* (Maryknoll, NY: Orbis Books, 1984), a luminous reflection on the spirituality of liberation of the church converted to the poor, draws for corroboration from Archbishop Romero more than from any other single source.

Romero, a timid, cautious conservative was appointed archbishop of San Salvador on February 28, 1977, at age fifty-nine. Within three weeks, the most pastoral and prophetic of his priests, Rutilio Grande, was assassinated. As the archbishop lifted his bullet-riddled body, a transposition occurred. It was the crucified Jesus whom he was embracing. Silently he pledged to his Lord that as Rutilio had followed him to the end, so would he. There began a ministry of joy and sorrow, of feeding multitudes with God's word, of angering the authorities, of building up messianic communities eager to receive the rule of God, and of denouncing the inevitable violence with which the unrepentant privileged resist the liberation of the captives. His ministry as prophet-pastor, like that of his Lord, lasted three years. Like his Lord, he was executed for endangering the established order. Like his Lord, he rose again to guarantee the resurrection of his people.

He did what all biblical prophets did before him. He proclaimed the will of God in direct challenge to the complex historical reality of the people, in painstaking dialogue with the social, the economic, the political, and the cultural. He, too, learned to apply the social sciences, mostly from what he learned from the hurts of his flock, but also from the theologians of the Catholic University, whose company he was not embarrassed to seek. Early in his tenure, he began to use the powerful Catholic radio station YSAX as his weekly national Sunday pulpit. His homilies were a blend of social analysis, Bible exposition, prophetic denunciation, and pastoral consolation.

As the homilies grew in length, eventually longer than an hour, so grew his audience, until the whole nation—friend, skeptic, and foe—gathered around the radio in an eerie ritual of Sunday electronic unity. The poor were galvanized by his announcement of the good news that in God's kingdom, now at hand, they were blessed, because they were no longer meant to be poor. The rich, the military, and the death squads listened, no doubt to hear whether there was hope for them too. And there was, but the price of such hope was too high: to share their lands, to pay equitable salaries, to release the innocent from prison, to let the workers unionize, to allow fair and free elections, to divert military expenditures to health, education, and housing. They heard themselves called repeatedly to conversion. Instead, they denounced him as subversive in their controlled media, bombed his radio station into silence several times, and sought further to terrorize him by a systematic campaign of tortures, disappearances, and executions against his followers. And eventually, they had him murdered.

His fellow bishops denounced him also, except for one, now his successor—Arturo Rivera y Damas. Their charge was that neither the church nor its pastors should take sides. One of those bishops was and is still the military vicar of the Salvadoran armed forces. Perhaps nothing pains Christian prophets more than the inevitable division that their

166

prophecy causes in the household of faith. Romero, the frail country priest with a history of bouts with the nerves for most of his adult life, was led in his anguish to tap the deepest levels of God's sustaining grace, a grace that he experienced more deeply still as he deepened his companionship with the least of Christ's brothers and sisters.

As we have seen, liberation theologians, from their pastoral involvement with the poor, have rehabilitated the notion of utopia. From Paulo Freire's pedagogical theory they have learned that only oppressed people can denounce and announce, that only they are capable of working out revolutionary utopias and not conservative or reformist ideologies. Utopia, for Freire, means that unblocking of the imagination in which a future possibility with the character of a realizable vision is perceived as a radical alternative to the present order. When, for the Christian poor, this utopian vision crosses the path of the kingdom of God promised by prophets and ushered by Jesus, the implications are revolutionary and immediately applicable to a situation of injustice. Add to this vision of future possibilities the certainty of the resurrection *in history* with Jesus, and one can realize the extraordinary potential for negating the present order in favor of one in which God is present with us, wiping away every tear from our eyes, letting death be no more, with no mourning or crying or pain, for the former things have passed away.

As a pastor, Oscar Romero learned to read the hope of the future in this way from his people, for whom the creed was becoming their faith. Nothing illustrates his own hope more luminously than the way he anticipated the assassination of his fellow prophets and his own. It is a fitting memorial to a pastor-prophet who not only denounced, but also announced. Two weeks before his martyrdom he said:

> I say it with no boasting, but rather with the greatest humility. If they kill me I will rise in the Salvadoran people. If the threats come about, as of now I offer my blood for the redemption of El Salvador. Let my blood be the seed of liberty and a

sign that our hopes may be soon realized, that my people may go free and that our hope in the future may be confirmed.[75]

At his funeral, after one and a half hours of horror caused by the firing of soldiers over the heads of more than one hundred thousand mourners gathered in front of the cathedral, and as some of us went around picking up the bodies of his friends killed by trampling and asphyxiation, I heard already kneeling around his crypt many of his friends praying to him for peace and justice. The pastor-prophet now sits with Jesus at the right hand of God, interceding for El Salvador. He intercedes also for us that our nation may share in the conversion of his people so that we may be allies and not enemies of the hope for which he lived and died.

Notes

Chapter 1. Prophetic Ministry

1. The following is a brief indication of the range of the contributions by representatives of the classic theological disciplines to the nature of the ministry of the church and, in particular, to the nature and scope of *pastoral* ministry since the mid-1970s: Bernard Cooke, *Ministry to Word and Sacrament* (Philadelphia: Fortress Press, 1978); James Fenhagen, *Mutual Ministry* and *Ministry and Solitude* (New York: Seabury Press, 1977, 1981, respectively); Thomas C. Oden, *Pastoral Theology* (San Francisco: Harper & Row, 1983); Edward Schillebeeckx, "A Creative Retrospect as Inspiration for the Ministry of the Future," in Lucas Grollenberg et al., *Minister, Pastor, Prophet* (New York: Crossroad, 1981). The reader is specially urged to consult the extensive bibliographies provided by Cooke and Oden.
2. Edward E. Thornton, *Professional Education for Ministry* (Nashville: Abingdon Press, 1970), chs. 1–2.
3. Helen Frances Dunbar, in Thornton, *Professional Education*, p. 37.
4. John S. Bonnell, *Pastoral Psychiatry* (New York: Harper & Bros., 1938).
5. Gote Bergsten, *Pastoral Psychology* (London: George Allen & Unwin, 1951). A further indication of the popularization of the term is found in *The Journal of Pastoral Psychology*.
6. Wayne E. Oates, *The Religious Dimensions of Personality* (New York: Association Press, 1957), p. vii.

169

7. Carroll A. Wise, *The Meaning of Pastoral Care* (New York: Harper & Row, 1966), pp. 86–87.

8. Ibid., p. 127.

9. William B. Oglesby Jr., "Heritage and Commitment: CPE in the Second Half Century," in *ACPE 1975 Conference Proceedings Fiftieth Anniversary of CPE* (New York: Association for Clinical Pastoral Education, 1975), pp. 84–89.

10. James A. Wharton, "Theology and Ministry in the Hebrew Scripture," in *A Biblical Basis for Ministry*, ed. Earl E. Shelp and Ronald Sunderland (Philadelphia: Westminster Press, 1981), pp. 18–19.

11. Donald Browning, "Pastoral Care and Public Ministry," *The Christian Century*, September 28, 1966, pp. 1176–77.

12. Ibid., p. 1176.

13. See Earl E. Shelp and Ronald Sunderland, "Introduction," *A Biblical Basis for Ministry*, pp. 11–16.

14. See O.S. Rankin, "Prophecy," in Alan Richardson, *A Theological Wordbook of the Bible* (New York: Macmillan, 1950), pp. 178–82.

15. R.B.Y. Scott, "Introduction and Exegesis, Isaiah chs. 1–39," in *The Interpreters' Bible* (Nashville: Abingdon Press, 1956), 5:284.

16. Ibid., 5:285.

17. Jürgen Moltmann and Douglas M. Meeks, "The Liberation of Oppressors," in *Christianity and Crisis*, December 25, 1978, p. 311.

18. Anthony Ugolnik, "The Godlessness Within: Stereotyping the Russians," in *The Christian Century*, November 9, 1983, p. 1011.

19. Maurice Simon, "Megillah: Translated into English with Notes," in *The Babylon Talmud Seder Mo'ed*, ed. I. Epstein (London: Soncio Press, 1938), 4:59.

20. Douglas Robinson, "Dr. King Proposes a Boycott of War," *New York Times*, April 4, 1967, p. 1.

21. National Conference of Catholic Bishops, *The Challenge of Peace: God's Promise and Our Response* (Washington, DC: U.S. Catholic Conference, 1983).

22. Ibid., p. iii.

23. Richard Halloran, "Bishops Challenge MX in Testimony," *New York Times*, June 27, 1984, p. 1.
24. National Conference of Catholic Bishops, *Challenge of Peace*, pp. 1–2.
25. Ibid., p. 17 (italics added).
26. Patrick G. Coy, "Martin Luther King, Jr., and the Catholic Bishops' Peace Letter," *The Christian Century*, April 4, 1984, p. 340.
27. Robert Reinhold, "Churches and U.S. Clash on Alien Sanctuary," *New York Times*, June 28, 1984, p. 1.
28. Ibid., p. 10.
29. Eric Jorstad, "A Theological Reflection on Sanctuary," *Christianity and Crisis*, October 31, 1983, p. 404. See also Eric Jorstad, "Sanctuary for Refugees: A Statement on Public Policy," *The Christian Century*, March 14, 1984, pp. 274–76.
30. Ibid., p. 406.
31. William D. Bedell, "Churchmen Drawing Fire in Tense Central America," *Houston Post*, July 27, 1981, p. 30.
32. Russell Chandler, "Clergy and Labor Fight for Jobless," *Los Angeles Times*, June 10, 1984, p. 1.
33. Ibid., p. 33.
34. Personal communication, June 3, 1984; quoted with permission.
35. Ibid. (italics added).
36. Chandler, "Clergy and Labor," p. 34. (Media attention appears to have shifted from the prophetic nature of the unionists' plea for the pastoral support of the religious community to the legal and ecclesiastical problems the Lutheran community has with one of its clergy. That may make for good copy for the morning TV news services, but it makes even more poignant the reported comments by von Waldow.)
37. Geoffrey Barker, "The Prime Minister and the Old Rugged Cross," *The Australian*, August 4, 1984, p. 12.
38. Ibid. (italics added).

Chapter 2. The Pastor as Prophet

1. Joseph Hough, "The Education of Practical Theologians," un-

published manuscript, p. 23. Hough's paper is a summary of a soon-to-be-published book that was jointly authored with John Cobb.

2. *Leaves from the Notebook of a Tamed Cynic* by Reinhold Niebuhr (New York: Meridian, 1960), p. 74. Copyright © 1929, renewed 1957 by Reinhold Niebuhr. Reprinted by permission of Harper & Row Publishers, Inc.

3. Ibid., pp. 128–29.

4. Ibid., p. 75.

5. There are hopeful signs that this split is being healed. For example, see the essays in *Practical Theology: The Emerging Field of Theology, Church, and World*, ed. Don Browning (San Francisco: Harper & Row, 1983). In his *Christian Century* (Feb. 1–8, 1984) article, "The Revival of Practical Theology," Browning says that he fears that the new emphasis on theology recovering a sense of *habitus* or *paideia* is that it will be too closely associated with the renewed interest in a theological ethic of virtue, character, and disposition (p. 141). Such an emphasis has some validity. Browning thinks that the corresponding emphasis on the Christian story as determinative for the depiction of the virtues fails to supply the publicly necessary principles to sustain the church's socially critical task. Thus, "a practical theology of virtue and character must be supplemented and supported by a practical theology of procedure and one, I believe, that also builds an important role for ethical principles in theological reflection" (p. 141). This is not the place to respond to these assumptions, but they are relevant to the subject of this paper to the extent that Browning's criticism seems to imply that an emphasis on virtue cannot sustain the kind of witness required of those who would be prophetic. Such a perspective, unfortunately, continues to underwrite the liberal presumptions that politics is not about the training of virtue and character. As a result, although an ethics of principle may appear to be more critical than an ethics of virtue, in fact it continues to underscore the limits of both our political experience and our theory. In the name of being publicly relevant, such a view fails decisively to be prophetic. For a critique of liberal political theory, that is, the ethos that determines what will count for our "public" ethics from the perspective I am suggesting, see

Michael Sandel, *Liberalism and the Limits of Justice* (Cambridge University Press, 1982).

6. Walter Rauschenbusch, *Christianity and the Social Crisis* (New York: Harper & Row, 1964). Used by permission.

7. Ibid., p. 3.

8. Ibid., p. 7.

9. Ibid., p. 9.

10. Ibid., p. 10.

11. Ibid., pp. 11–12.

12. Ibid., pp. 13–14.

13. Ibid., p. 16.

14. Ibid., p. 16.

15. Ibid., p. 25.

16. Ibid., p. 27–28.

17. Ibid., pp. 30–31.

18. For a critique of these assumptions that have dominated so much of the study of Hebrew scripture, see Joseph Blenkinsopp, "Old Testament Theology and the Jewish-Christian Connection," *Journal of the Study of the Old Testament* 28 (1984):3–15. Although it is difficult to prove, one cannot help but believe that our failure to appreciate the "sectarian" form of later prophecy derives partly from our inability to see the church in tension with our social order. We turn the prophets into social critics in the name of securing justice within our social assumptions. We do not, however, take the risk of thinking the prophets might well call into question the very basis of our social order, such as challenging the assumption that democracy and the national purpose legitimated in its name may fundamentally be idolatrous.

19. Joseph Blenkinsopp, *A History of Prophecy in Israel* (Philadelphia: Westminster Press, 1983), p. 40.

20. Ibid., p. 90.

21. Gerhard von Rad, *Old Testament Theology*, vol. 2 (New York: Harper & Row, 1965). For von Rad's particular emphasis, see his account of "The Prophets' Conception of the Word of God," pp. 80–98.

22. Blenkinsopp, *History of Prophecy*, p. 38. Rauschenbusch's account of the prophets was in reaction to the equally distorted understanding of the prophets primarily as foretellers of the

future—and in particular, Jesus. The prophets certainly were not simply predictors of the future, but neither can that side of prophecy be ignored. Particularly if, as I shall emphasize below, we stress the significance of interpretation of history as definitive of the prophetic task.

23. John Howard Yoder, *Preface to Theology: Christology and Theological Method* (Elkhart, IN: Goshen Biblical Seminary, 1982), pp. 246–47. Unfortunately, I have not had a chance to read Walter Brueggemann's book *The Prophetic Imagination* (Philadelphia: Fortress Press, 1978), but his thesis seems compatible with the one suggested here. In a review of the book, Kent Richard quotes Brueggemann's thesis: "The task of prophetic ministry is to nurture, nourish, and to evoke a consciousness in perception alternative to the consciousness and perception of the dominant culture around us" (*Christian Century*, May 23, 1979, p. 593).

24. Blenkinsopp, *History of Prophecy*, p. 256.

25. Ibid., p. 257.

26. Yoder, *Preface to Theology*, p. 248.

27. For a fuller presentation of the ideas in the paragraph, see my *A Community of Character: Toward a Constructive Christian Social Ethic* (Notre Dame, IN: University of Notre Dame Press, 1981).

28. I happened to mention to my pastor that I was working on this paper, and I hoped in a way that would overcome the split between the pastoral and prophetic. In response, he told a story that nicely illustrates the perspective I have been trying to develop. He said that he had just left visiting one of our elderly parishioners who was deeply concerned that after ten years he was changing churches. She was particularly concerned that he should come back to bury her. He had told her he had no intention of doing so and he thought that was a prophetic act. I think he was right, for in refusing to return to bury her, he reminded her that it is not this or that pastor that makes the church the church, but God present through this historic and particular group of people. By refusing to bury her, he was reminding her of the story that sustained her and all Christians as we face death.

29. James Lapsley has recently objected to Don Browning's at-

tempt to understand pastoral theology as a branch of ethics, "because ethics is focused upon norms and goals as its primary concern, and because much pastoral care is only tangentially related to ethics in any developed sense of the term. Rather the 'cup of cold water' extended in a personal relationship is generic to the gospel itself. To be sure, ethical and even disciplinary questions do explicitly arise in pastoral care (the latter when there is a 'clear and present danger' to self or others), but in these instances the theologically discerned possibilities retain status as criteria" ("Practical Theology and Pastoral Care: An Essay in Pastoral Theology," in *Pastoral Theology*, ed. Don Browning [Philadelphia: Fortress Press, 1983], p. 170). Lapsley's limited account of ethics prevents him from seeing that his very understanding of what constitutes a "pastoral situation" already assumes a normative stance. As a result, he fails to see that even when we begin with "suffering persons," we cannot help but try to enable them to bring their suffering in contact with the story of the gospel.

30. In his *Pastoral Theology: Essentials of Ministry* (San Francisco: Harper & Row, 1983), Thomas Oden has presented an account of the ministry that attempts to restore integrity to the ministerial office. He does so, however, by insisting that all the varied activities of the pastor must have a single center life—life in Christ. When clergy are disconnected from this historic identity and "from the history of revelation and the capacity of God to address the heart, they easily become too cheaply accommodative to the present culture and lose the finely balanced judgment that the tradition has called wisdom" (p. 55).

31. Some may think that this example necessarily presupposes a negative attitude toward abortion; I do not think this is the case. Although I have argued elsewhere that abortion as a practice cannot be seen as a "good" by Christians, my depiction of this case does not depend on that analysis. Rather, all that is presupposed is the woman's own general feeling that abortion, all other things being equal, is not "a good thing." What I do think this example exhibits is the low state of moral discourse in many Protestant churches about such matters. Generally, Protestants have simply accepted our society's unthinking liberalism about abortion and the place of children in general. As a result, we

175

flounder as pastors, since we cannot draw on any set of moral convictions to help people guide their lives. If such cases tell us anything, it is that we cannot avoid making these kinds of matters subjects that we must confront if the church is to make any pretense of being, in James Gustafson's memorable phrase, a community of moral discourse.

Chapter 3. The Prophet as a Destabilizing Presence

1. For current statements on the inclinations of scholarship, see the excellent books by Joseph Blenkinsopp, *A History of Prophecy in Israel* (Philadelphia: Westminster Press, 1983), and Klaus Koch, *The Prophets; The Assyrian Age* (Philadelphia: Fortress Press, 1982).
2. At the present time, the definitive book on the subject is Robert R. Wilson, *Prophecy and Society in Ancient Israel* (Philadelphia: Fortress Press, 1980). Scholars are increasingly noticing that as one talks about "organizations of society," one may observe that a variety of things can be "organized" in partisan ways. Note two suggestive titles by Bernhard Lang, "The Social Organization of Peasant Poverty in Biblical Israel" (*Journal of the Study of the Old Testament* 24 [1982]:47–63), and by Gary Alan Herion, "The Social Organization of Tradition in Monarchic Judah" (unpublished dissertation, University of Michigan, 1982).
3. See my paper, "A Shape for Old Testament Theology. 1: Structure Legitimation," *Catholic Biblical Quarterly* (in press).
4. I have explored some of the implications of this in *The Prophetic Imagination* (Philadelphia: Fortress Press, 1978).
5. A. Vanlier Hunter, *Seek the Lord* (Baltimore: St. Mary's Seminary and University, 1982), has demonstrated that consistently the prophets do not appeal for repentance. What appears to be such an appeal is characteristically reference to an earlier appeal that has been rejected. The old appeal for repentance regularly leads to a conclusion of judgment. In the present form of the prophetic text, it is the speech of judgment that overrides every possibility of serious repentance.
6. Among the important studies of the Elijah narratives are the

following: L. Bronner, *The Stories of Elijah and Elisha* (Pretoria Oriental Series, vol. 6; Leiden: E.J. Brill, 1968); Georg Fohrer, *Elia* (ATANT 53; Zurich: Zwingli Verlag, 1968); O. Steck, "Uberlieferung und Zeitgeschichte in den Elia-Ergangungen," (WMANT 26; Neukirchen-Vluyn: Neukirchener Verlag, 1968); and R.S. Wallace, *Elijah and Elisha* (London: Oliver and Boyd, 1957). Two books that are not so critically disciplined, but that are important for the sort of argument made here are Jacques Ellul, *The Politics of God and the Politics of Man* (Grand Rapids, MI: Eerdmans, 1972), and Davie Napier, *Word of God, Word of Earth* (New York: United Church Press, 1976).

7. See my expository comments in *I Kings* (Atlanta: John Knox Press, 1982) and *II Kings* (Atlanta: John Knox Press, 1982).

8. The most important impetus in this direction comes from canonical criticism, especially the work of Brevard Childs, *Introduction to the Old Testament as Scripture* (Philadelphia: Fortress Press, 1979), but it also reflects the increasing importance of literary theory for Old Testament study.

9. See the discerning analysis of R. D. Laing, *The Politics of the Family and Other Essays* (New York: Pantheon Books, 1971).

10. Erhard Gerstenberger, *Der bittende Mensch: Bittritual und Klagelied des Einzelmen im Alten Testament* (Neukirchen-Vluyn: Neukirchener Verlag, 1980), pp. 107–69, has argued that Israel had ways in which to conduct "liturgies of rehabilitation," even though these escape our rationality of modernity. Perhaps the work of Elijah here is in the context and according to the accepted form of such an enterprise.

11. See the striking statement of Ellul, "Meditation of Inutility," *Politics of God,* pp. 190–99. Ellul's analysis concerns the inutility of human effort, but the implied counterpart that resonates with Ellul's analysis is the inutility of God for every human agenda.

12. See my article "'Impossibility' and Epistemology in the Faith Tradition of Abraham and Sarah (Gen. 18:1–15)," *Zeitschrift für die Alttestamentiche Wissenschaft* 94 (1982):615–34.

13. Robert B. Coote, *Amos Among the Prophets* (Philadelphia: Fortress Press, 1981) pp. 24–45, has well summarized the data from a sociologic perspective.

Chapter 4. The Prophetic Task of Pastoral Ministry

1. For further reading, see Donald Kraybill, *The Upside-Down Kingdom* (Scottdale, PA: Herald Press, 1978); John H. Yoder, *The Politics of Jesus* (Grand Rapids, MI: Eerdmans, 1972); and John H. Yoder, *The Priestly Kingdom* (Notre Dame, IN: University of Notre Dame Press, 1985).

Chapter 5. Paul, Prophet and Spiritual Leader

1. Adolf Deissmann, *Light from the Ancient East*, trans. Lionel R.M. Strachan (New York: Hodder & Stoughton, 1910).
2. See, for example, Victor Paul Furnish, "Theology and Ministry in the Pauline Letters," in *A Biblical Basis for Ministry*, ed. Earl E. Shelp and Ronald Sunderland (Philadelphia: Westminster Press, 1981), pp. 101–44, 234–36.
3. Cf. the article "Prophet," by Carl Heinz Peisker and Colin Brown, in *The New International Dictionary of the New Testament* (Grand Rapids, MI: Zondervan, 1978), 3:74–92, with extensive bibliography; also the article "prophētēs," by G. Friedrich et al., in *Theological Dictionary of the New Testament* (Grand Rapids, MI: Eerdmans, 1968), 6:781–861.
4. The text of this verse is uncertain; some ancient manuscripts do not contain "a command." Whichever reading one adopts does not affect the argument here.
5. "Sentences of Holy Law in the New Testament," conveniently available in Käsemann's *New Testament Questions of Today* (Philadelphia: Fortress Press, 1969), pp. 66–81.
6. See, for example, Peisker and Brown, "Prophet," pp. 84–86.

Chapter 6. The Passion of God and the Prophetic Task of Pastoral Ministry

1. John Calvin, *Institutes of the Christian Religion*, ed. John T. McNeill (Philadelphia: Westminster Press, 1960), 1:35–39.
2. Dorothee Soelle, *Suffering* (Philadelphia: Fortress Press, 1975), p. 39.
3. Ibid., p. 38.
4. Ibid., p. 4.

5. Abraham Heschel, *The Prophets* (New York: Harper & Row, 1962).
6. Cf. Jürgen Moltmann, *The Crucified God* (New York: Harper & Row, 1974).
7. Johann Baptist Metz, *Faith in History and Society* (New York: Seabury Press, 1980), p. 201.
8. *The Pittsburgh Press,* May 7, 1984.
9. See Dennis P. McCann, "Practical Theology and Social Action: Or What Can the 1980s Learn from the 1960s?" in *Practical Theology: Emerging Field in Theology, Church and World,* ed. Don S. Browning (San Francisco: Harper & Row, 1983), p. 109.
10. Ibid., p. 120.
11. See Daniel L. Migliore, *The Power of God* (Philadelphia: Westminster Press, 1983).

Chapter 7. Latin-American Liberation Theology

1. The best introduction to the person and work of Gustavo Gutiérrez is Robert McAfee Brown, *Gustavo Gutiérrez,* Makers of Contemporary Theology Series (Atlanta: John Knox Press, 1980). Of course, the indispensable volume to understand Gutiérrez' own work is his *A Theology of Liberation,* ed. and trans. Sister Caridad Inda and John Eagleson (Maryknoll, NY: Orbis Books, 1973), now in its tenth edition in English. (It has been translated into ten languages.) See also, among other volumes by him published by Orbis, *The Power of the Poor in History* (1983) and *We Drink from Our Own Wells* (1984).
2. With some adaptations, this historical overview is taken from Jorge Lara-Braud, *What Is Liberation Theology?* (Atlanta: Presbyterian Publishing House, 1980), pp. 7–13.
3. For a compact history of three and a half centuries of background for liberation theology in Latin America, see Enrique Dussell, *History and the Theology of Liberation* (Maryknoll, NY: Orbis Books, 1976).
4. See Rubem Alves, "Utopia Becomes Ideology," in *Our Claim on the Future,* ed. Jorge Lara-Braud (New York: Friendship Press, 1970), pp. 62–78.
5. See the classic study on Chilean Pentecostalism in Christian

Lalive d'Epinay, *Haven of the Masses* (London: Lutterworth Press, 1969).

6. See Jacques Maritain, *True Humanism* (New York: Charles Scribner's Sons, 1938).
7. For an account of this process, see Gutiérrez, *Theology of Liberation,* pp. 53–72, and José Míguez Bonino, *Doing Theology in a Revolutionary Situation* (Philadelphia: Fortress Press, 1975).
8. Gutiérrez, *Theology of Liberation,* p. 30. Used by permission.
9. Nos. 9 and 85. Text of the official version found in *The Gospel of Peace and Justice: Catholic School Teaching Since Pope John,* ed. Joseph Gremillion (Maryknoll, NY: Orbis Books, 1975). This is a rich collection of official documents, including encyclicals, Medellín texts, and papal speeches.
10. Ibid., Nos. 10 and 20.
11. This point is made by Juan Luis Segundo, *The Liberation of Theology* (Maryknoll, NY: Orbis Books, 1975), p. 193.
12. The official English translation is published as *The Church in the Present-Day Transformation of Latin America in the Light of the Council;* vol. 1: *Position Papers;* vol. 2: *Conclusions,* ed. Louis Michael Colonnese (Washington, DC: Latin-American Division of the U.S. Catholic Conference, 1970). Hereinafter it will be referred to as *Medellín,* citing the document by title and paragraph number from vol. 2 (Conclusions). The texts of "Justice," "Peace," "Family and Demography," and "Poverty" are found in their entirety in *The Gospel of Peace and Justice.*
13. *Medellín,* "Peace," No. 14.
14. Ibid., No. 16.
15. *Medellín,* "Poverty," Nos. 1, 2, and 7.
16. Ibid., No. 10.
17. *Medellín,* "Justice," No. 3.
18. Ibid., No. 5. The quotation is from *Gaudium et Spes,* No. 39.
19. Ibid., No. 10.
20. *Medellín,* "Justice," No. 1.
21. See the most sympathetic treatment of the mutual challenge between Christians and Marxists, at least from a Protestant liberation theology in Latin America: José Míguez Bonino, *Christians and Marxists* (Grand Rapids, MI: Eerdmans, 1976), pp. 87–91. Also Gutiérrez, *Theology of Liberation,* pp. 88–92.

22. Míguez Bonino, *Christians and Marxists*, pp. 8, 19–23, analyzing the Chilean "third way."

23. This case is amply documented by Alan Preston Neely, a former Southern Baptist missionary, in his 1977 unpublished Ph.D. dissertation for American University, Washington, DC, entitled *Protestant Antecedents of the Latin American Theology of Liberation.* The most noted ISAL thinkers besides Shaull and Alves were José Míguez Bonino, Emilio Castro, Julio de Santa Ana, Sergio Arce, Christian Lalive, Leopoldo Niilus, Luis Odell, Gonzalo Castillo, Hiber Conteris, Pierre Furter, and, toward the end, Hugo Assmann. See also Míguez Bonino, *Doing Theology*, pp. 54–56.

24. See the Latin-American contributions to that conference in Paul Abrecht and M.M. Thomas, eds., *World Conference on Church and Society* (Geneva: World Council of Churches, 1967).

25. See Johannes B. Metz, *Theology of the World* (New York: Herder and Herder, 1969).

26. See Jürgen Moltmann's landmark volume, *Theology of Hope* (New York: Harper & Row, 1967).

27. The English version of the official report is Jorge Lara-Braud, trans., *Social Justice and the Latin Churches* (Atlanta: John Knox Press, 1969). See especially pp. 9–19 for a summary view of the radicalization of perspectives from 1961 to 1966.

28. Míguez Bonino, *Doing Theology in a Revolutionary Situation*, p. 55. He is referring to Alves' Princeton Seminary doctoral dissertation, published as *A Theology of Human Hope* (Washington, DC: Corpus Books, 1969).

29. C. Peter Wagner, *Latin American Theology: Radical or Evangelical* (Grand Rapids, MI: Eerdmans, 1970).

30. Ibid., p. 23. For calling attention to these arguments, I am indebted to Segundo's *Liberation of Theology*. He wishes Roman Catholic authorities would be as candid, especially because he suspects they attack liberation theology from a quite similar position (p. 138).

31. Ibid., p. 26.

32. Ibid., pp. 29–30.

33. Ibid., p. 32.

34. Ibid., p. 42.

181

35. Ibid., p. 55.
36. Quoted in Robert McAfee Brown, *Theology in a New Key* (Philadelphia: Westminster Press, 1978), p. 93. The biographical details are extracted from German Guzmán, *Camilo Torres* (New York: Sheed and Ward, 1969), and from a lucid summary of his life in Bonino, *Doing Theology*, pp. 43–44.
37. "La fuerza histórica de los pobres," an introduction to a collection of testimonials of the struggle of the Church in Latin America during the years 1973 through 1978 entitled *Signos de lucha y esperanza* (Lima: CEP, 1978).
38. *Signos de renovación*, 1969, in its English translation has been published as *Between Honesty and Hope* (Maryknoll, NY: Maryknoll Publications, 1970). The other, as yet untranslated, is *Signos de liberacion* (Lima: CEP, 1973). It covers the years from 1969 to 1973.
39. John Eagleson and Philip Scharper, *Puebla and Beyond* (the major addresses of John Paul II in Mexico, the Official Translation of the Final Puebla Document and Commentaries by R.M. Brown, Virgilio Elizondo, Joseph Gremillion, Penny Lernoux, Carlos McGrath, Moisés Sandoval and Jon Sobrino) (Maryknoll, NY: Orbis Books, 1979), No. 1134. Cf. nos. 1157, 1158.
40. Gutiérrez contrasts Latin-American theology and the "progressivist" theology of Europe in Sergio Torres and Virginia Fabella, *The Emergent Gospel: Theology from the Underside of History* (Maryknoll, NY: Orbis Books, 1976). See his essay "Two Theological Perspectives: Liberation Theology and Progressivist Theology," pp. 227–59.
41. Ernesto Cardenal, *The Gospel in Solentiname*, 4 vols. (Maryknoll, NY: Orbis Books, 1976–82).
42. Jon Sobrino, *Christology at the Crossroads* (Maryknoll, NY: Orbis Books, 1978).
43. Míguez Bonino, *Christians and Marxists*, pp. 91–94.
44. Brown, *Theology in a New Key*, pp. 88–97. Brown expands on these themes in his latest book, *Unexpected News: Reading the Bible with Third World Eyes* (Philadelphia: Westminster Press, 1984).
45. José Porfirio Miranda, *Marx and the Bible: A Critique of the Philosophy of Oppression* (Maryknoll, NY: Orbis Books, 1974).

By him, also published by Orbis, see *Marx Against the Marxists: The Christian Humanism of Karl Marx* (1980).

46. Míguez Bonino, *Christians and Marxists*, pp. 96–97.
47. Miranda, *Marx and the Bible*, pp. 84, 136.
48. Ismael García, *The Concept of Justice in Latin American Theology of Liberation*, unpublished doctoral dissertation, University of Chicago, December 1982, p. 147.
49. Gutiérrez, *Theology of Liberation*, p. 235. Used by permission.
50. See the issues of September 17, October 15, and November 26. The rebuttal was made by Rubem Alves, Archie LeMone, John C. Bennett, Robert McAfee Brown, Jacques Kazub, Thomas Quigley, and Alexander Wilde. Taking Sanders' position also was John Plank.
51. Gutiérrez, *Theology of Liberation*, pp. 28–32. Used by permission.
52. Letty M. Russell, *Human Liberation in a Feminine Perspective* (Philadelphia: Westminster Press, 1974), p. 45.
53. James H. Cone, *The God of the Oppressed* (New York: Seabury Press, 1975), p. 150.
54. Ibid., p. 132.
55. Gutiérrez, *Theology of Liberation*, p. 235. Used by permission.
56. Ibid., p. 237.
57. Ibid., p. 238.
58. Ibid., p. 35.
59. Ibid., p. 37.
60. Shubert Ogden, *Faith and Freedom: Toward a Theology of Liberation* (Nashville: Abingdon Press, 1979), pp. 36–37, 53.
61. Míguez Bonino, *Christians and Marxists*, pp. 138–40. Also Miranda, *Marx and the Bible*, p. 177. The failure of Marxism to deal with death is forcefully stated by Hugo Assmann, *Theology for a Nomad Church* (Maryknoll, NY: Orbis Books, 1975), p. 144. The original, *Opresión-Liberación* (Montevideo: Tierra Nueva, 1971), is considerably longer than the English version.
62. Gutiérrez, *Theology of Liberation*, p. 176 (italics added). Used by permission.
63. Ibid., p. 149.
64. Ibid., p. 151.
65. Ibid., p. 151.

66. Ibid., p. 151.
67. Ibid., p. 152. See Assmann's *Theology for a Nomad Church,* chs. 1 and 4. Juan Luis Segundo observes that Vatican II, especially in *Gaudium et Spes* (No. 22), legitimates the doctrine of a single history and protects those who expand its political implications from heterodoxy. See his *Liberation of Theology* (Maryknoll, NY: Orbis Books, 1976), p. 141.
68. In Rossino Gibellini, ed., *Frontiers of Theology in Latin America* (Maryknoll, NY: Orbis Books, 1979), p. 267. Míguez Bonino expands the argument in *Doing Theology,* pp. 132–52.
69. Gibellini, *Frontiers,* p. 266.
70. Gutiérrez, *Theology of Liberation,* p. 157. Used by permission.
71. Segundo, *Liberation of Theology,* p. 144.
72. Ibid., p. 145.
73. A valuable reflection on prophetism as it applies to Latin America, unfortunately not yet translated into English, is *Misión Profética de la Iglesia* (various Latin-American authors) (Mexico City: Casa Unida de Publicaciones, 1981).
74. There are two biographies of Romero in English. Plácido Erdozaín, *Archbishop Romero: Martyr of Salvador* (lengthy introduction by Jorge Lara-Braud) (Maryknoll, NY: Orbis Books, 1980). The other is a masterpiece: James R. Brockman, *The Word Remains: A Life of Oscar Romero* (Maryknoll, NY: Orbis Books, 1983). Brockman has just published (1984) a collection of memorable quotes, mostly from the archbishop's homilies: *The Church Is All of You* (Minneapolis: Winston Press, 1984). The composite picture I draw of Oscar Romero in this paper is taken from these volumes, but principally from my personal acquaintance with him.
75. My translation from Jon Sobrino, *Mons. Romero: Verdadero Profeta* (Bilbao, Spain: Editorial Desclee de Brouwer, 1982), pp. 138–39.